The Early Middle Ages

Other Books in the Turning Points Series:

Turning|
|Points
IN WORLD HISTORY

The Early Middle Ages

Jeff Hay, *Book Editor*

David L. Bender, *Publisher*
Bruno Leone, *Executive Editor*
Bonnie Szumski, *Editorial Director*
Stuart B. Miller, *Managing Editor*

Greenhaven Press, Inc., San Diego, California

Library of Congress Cataloging-in-Publication Data

The Early Middle Ages / Jeff Hay, book editor.
    p.   cm. — (Turning points in world history)
    Includes bibliographical references and index.
    ISBN 0-7377-0481-0 (pbk. : alk. paper) —
ISBN 0-7377-0482-9 (lib. bdg. : alk. paper)
    1. Civilization, Medieval. 2. Europe, History—476–1492.
3. Military art and science—History—Medieval, 500–1500.
4. Europe—Church history—600–1500. I. Hay, Jeff. II. Turning
points in world history (Greenhaven Press).

D121 .E27 2001
909.07—dc21
                                                        00-034110
                                                             CIP

Cover photo: Scala/Art Resource
Dover: 171
North Wind Picture Archives: 19, 21, 30, 32, 46, 87, 108, 144
Prints Old and Rare: 17

© 2001 by Greenhaven Press, Inc.
P.O. Box 289009, San Diego, CA 92198-9009

Printed in the U.S.A.

Contents

Chapter 2: The German and Hun Invasions

Chapter 3: The Byzantine Empire and Eastern Orthodox Christianity

Charlemagne reestablished the Roman Empire in western Europe.

Chapter 5: The Early Middle Ages Give Way to the High Middle Ages

Foreword

Certain past events stand out as pivotal, as having effects and outcomes that change the course of history. These events are often referred to as turning points. Historian Louis L. Snyder provides this useful definition:

> A turning point in history is an event, happening, or stage which thrusts the course of historical development into a different direction. By definition a turning point is a great event, but it is even more—a great event with the explosive impact of altering the trend of man's life on the planet.

History's turning points have taken many forms. Some were single, brief, and shattering events with immediate and obvious impact. The invasion of Britain by William the Conqueror in 1066, for example, swiftly transformed that land's political and social institutions and paved the way for the rise of the modern English nation. By contrast, other single events were deemed of minor significance when they occurred, only later recognized as turning points. The assassination of a little-known European nobleman, Archduke Franz Ferdinand, on June 28, 1914, in the Bosnian town of Sarajevo was such an event; only after it touched off a chain reaction of political-military crises that escalated into the global conflict known as World War I did the murder's true significance become evident.

Other crucial turning points occurred not in terms of a few hours, days, months, or even years, but instead as evolutionary developments spanning decades or even centuries. One of the most pivotal turning points in human history, for instance—the development of agriculture, which replaced nomadic hunter-gatherer societies with more permanent settlements—occurred over the course of many generations. Still other great turning points were neither events nor developments, but rather revolutionary new inventions and innovations that significantly altered social customs and ideas, military tactics, home life, the spread of knowledge, and the human condition in general. The developments of writing, gunpowder, the printing press, antibiotics, the electric light, atomic energy, television, and the computer, the last two of which have recently ushered in the world-altering information age, represent only some of these innovative turning points.

Each anthology in the Greenhaven Turning Points in World History series presents a group of essays chosen for their accessibility. The anthology's structure also enhances this accessibility. First, an introductory essay provides a general overview of the principal events and figures involved, placing the topic in its historical context. The essays that follow explore various aspects in more detail, some targeting political trends and consequences, others social, literary, cultural, and/or technological ramifications, and still others pivotal leaders and other influential figures. To aid the reader in choosing the material of immediate interest or need, each essay is introduced by a concise summary of the contributing writer's main themes and insights.

In addition, each volume contains extensive research tools, including a collection of excerpts from primary source documents pertaining to the historical events and figures under discussion. In the anthology on the French Revolution, for example, readers can examine the works of Rousseau, Voltaire, and other writers and thinkers whose championing of human rights helped fuel the French people's growing desire for liberty; the French *Declaration of the Rights of Man and Citizen*, presented to King Louis XVI by the French National Assembly on October 2, 1789; and eyewitness accounts of the attack on the royal palace and the horrors of the Reign of Terror. To guide students interested in pursuing further research on the subject, each volume features an extensive bibliography, which for easy access has been divided into separate sections by topic. Finally, a comprehensive index allows readers to scan and locate content efficiently. Each of the anthologies in the Greenhaven Turning Points in World History series provides students with a complete, detailed, and enlightening examination of a crucial historical watershed.

Introduction

Western Europe was only sparsely populated when the Roman Empire began expanding northward from its Italian base in the first and second centuries B.C. The main inhabitants were Germanic and Celtic tribes who lived in small, seminomadic groups. There were no roads, no towns, and very little trade or culture. Indeed, there was no hint, as the Roman Empire conquered and incorporated western Europe, that the region would eventually develop a unique, coherent civilization. The main focus of the Roman world, after all, was in Italy itself as well as areas of the Mediterranean and Near East, such as Greece, Egypt, and Palestine, with rich and ancient cultures. Western Europe, by comparison, was a backwater.

A distinctly western European civilization did, however, ultimately emerge. It was very different not only from Rome but from the ancient Near East, although aspects of its origins could be traced to both. Western European civilization began in the period known as the Early Middle Ages.

The Early Middle Ages is the first half or so of what historians refer to as the medieval era or, simply, Middle Ages. Opinions on its extent differ, but the Early Middle Ages can be dated from approximately A.D. 324, when the Roman emperor Constantine established a new imperial capital at Constantinople, to 1000, when the High, or Late, Middle Ages began.

Historians sometimes refer to the Early Middle Ages as the Dark Ages. Indeed, by comparison with Rome at its height or the revived European civilization of the Renaissance of the 1400s and 1500s, the period was indeed dark. Population declined along with city life. Trade and manufacturing virtually ceased. Culture and literacy, outside of narrow church circles, scarcely existed. Even worse, violence, warfare, and disease were the constant companions of Europeans during the Early Middle Ages.

Underneath this rather grim surface, however, a distinct

culture was taking shape. Christianity continued to spread to unconverted populations. This helped not only give life a religious focus, but create a unified culture. All western Christians not only followed the same rituals, they obeyed the head of the church, the pope. In many ways the papacy was the most powerful institution of the era.

The monastic movement also expanded the reach of the church. In fact, monasteries replaced towns during the Early Middle Ages. Not only did they serve religious functions, they also operated as administrative, economic, and educational centers.

The church hierarchy sometimes worked in tandem with the Germanic kings. Germanic kingdoms, thanks in part to lessons from Rome, had emerged as the most powerful political entities in western Europe after Rome fell. Germanic culture, based in part on the importance of kinship ties as well as success in war, was to be a fundamental part of the developing European culture. Among the important legacies of Germanic Europe was the feudal system, which divided Europe into a complicated hierarchy of landowning nobles. To this day, many Europeans claim descent from the kings, princes, counts, and dukes of the feudal era.

Growing division between western Europe and the Near East was yet another factor that helped western civilization develop its distinct identity. Even after Rome fell to Germanic warriors in 476, the Roman Empire was kept alive at its new capital, Constantinople (modern-day Istanbul); later known as the Byzantine Empire, it endured until 1453. For much of that era Byzantine emperors claimed authority over western Europe, and the Byzantines developed their own unique version of Christianity. But western Europeans refused to accept the authority of the Byzantines, preferring the leadership of the popes and Germanic kings such as Charlemagne. By 1000, the split between east and west was virtually complete, and has largely remained so.

Turning Points: The Early Middle Ages provides an introduction to this multifaceted era, when Roman traditions, the early Christian Church, and the Germanic kingdoms combined to create a culture that dominated Europe for many centuries.

A Brief History of the Early Middle Ages

On Christmas Day in the year 800, Charlemagne, the king of the Franks, was in Rome. Already, Charlemagne's military successes had allowed him to enlarge his kingdom to include much of western Europe. In addition, Charlemagne had shown himself to be the defender of the Roman Catholic Church by stopping Muslim incursions and by protecting Pope Leo III, the head of the church, from his enemies.

Surrounded by bishops, abbots, and Roman elders, Leo approached Charlemagne as the king said a prayer in front of the tomb of St. Peter. When the prayer was finished, Leo placed a crown on Charlemagne's head and proclaimed him Holy Roman Emperor, the descendant of the Caesars of Rome. To the east, the Byzantine emperors claimed that honor. But Charlemagne and Leo had in mind a new empire, a political and religious alliance that would signify the emergence of a new civilization.

The new civilization was Western Europe, a combination of Roman traditions, Roman Catholic Christianity, and Frankish and Germanic customs such as feudal honor and fealty. Its character developed throughout the period known as the Early Middle Ages, which historians date from approximately A.D. 324 to 1000. Christmas Day 800, the year of Charlemagne's coronation, was its culminating moment.

The Fall of the Roman Empire

The Roman Empire of antiquity reached its height during the first and second centuries A.D., a period known as the Pax Romana, or Roman Peace. During this period the Empire reached its greatest extent, stretching from the modern Middle East to the British Isles in the west. Its navies completely controlled the Mediterranean Sea. Its emperors ruled peacefully over large and diverse populations, and wealth flowed into the capital at a rapid and regular rate.

During the third century, however, the Empire underwent a series of crises from which it never recovered. A crucial threat came from new enemies. A strong Persian Empire governed by the Sassanid dynasty began to chip away at Rome's eastern possessions. In western Europe, the Germanic tribes that had inhabited those regions before the Romans arrived grew more aggressive and more envious of Rome's wealth. One tribe in particular, the Goths, began to penetrate Roman territory by A.D. 250, threatening its northern borders. Other so-called barbarian tribes, encouraged by the success of the Goths, wanted to try their own luck against their Roman overlords.

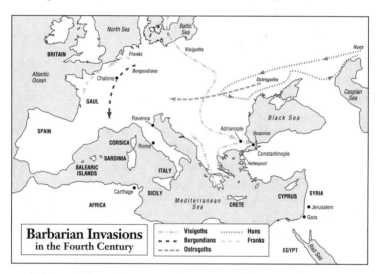

Barbarian Invasions in the Fourth Century

The Roman Empire had become weak internally as well, making it easier for outsiders such as the barbarian tribes and Persians to attack. The Roman army was ragged and badly led, money was short, social revolts threatened, and political instability led to a rapid turnover of emperors, particularly in the third century. By 284, in fact, Rome was torn by civil war.

The emperors Diocletian (284–305) and Constantine (306–337) managed to stabilize the Empire for a short time. This stabilization, however, came at a high price as Diocletian and Constantine had to introduce a system of absolute imperial control. The emperor ruled by decree, rather than

by consulting with advisers, and depended on a large bureaucracy to carry out his will. In addition, and unlike most
earlier Roman emperors, Diocletian and Constantine lived
aloof from their subjects, claiming that their right to rule
came from the gods. Constantine in particular exaggerated
his exalted status; visitors who came before him were required to kneel and kiss the hem of his purple robe.

As the Roman Empire suffered chaos and decline in the
third, fourth, and fifth centuries, Christianity grew attractive
to ever greater numbers of people. They were attracted by
its theology, which promised salvation to all as well as a personal relationship with God. But they were also drawn to the
stability and security that Christian communities offered.

The Rise of Christianity

The Christian religion sprang from the ancient Near East in
the first century A.D. It expanded rapidly, particularly in the
eastern part of the Roman Empire. Despite rare instances of
persecution, Roman leaders did not find Christianity to be a
threat in this early period. Christians were simply one of
many religious minorities throughout the Empire, whose official policy was religious toleration.

By the mid–third century, in fact, Christianity had grown
sufficiently strong and widespread that Roman leaders were
forced to recognize its influence. Over time, its adherents
had been more or less tolerated or persecuted: now, in an effort to revive the old pagan religion, Diocletian confiscated
church lands, banned Christian practices, and punished
Christians with imprisonment, torture, and exile. His methods, however, created further sympathy for Christians.

Constantine, well aware of the power of Christianity, as
well as the wealth and territory controlled by certain Christians in the east, enacted significant political and religious
reforms. In 313 the Edict of Milan, which declared religious
toleration throughout the Empire, was issued jointly by
Constantine and his coemperor, Licentius.

Constantine's reforms included the creation of a new imperial capital. The new center of Roman power was to be an
ancient Greek city known as Byzantium, which the emperor

Pope Leo III places a crown on Charlemagne, king of the Franks, and proclaims him Holy Roman Emperor on Christmas Day 800.

renamed Constantinople in 324. The city's location was its greatest advantage. It stood astride traditional trade routes between Europe and Asia, and was well situated for the defense of the richer eastern portion of the empire. In addition, it was easy to defend, unlike Rome itself. Constantinople was surrounded by water on three sides; to the east lay the Black Sea, to the west the Adriatic and Mediterranean, and separating the city from the Asian continent lay a narrow passage known as the Bosphorus. (Not until 1453 were Constantinople's defenses finally breached, and the city's period as the capital of the Roman Empire brought to an end.)

Moreover, Constantine was the first Roman emperor to convert to Christianity. He was officially baptized on his deathbed in Constantinople in 337. Later in the century Theodosius, emperor from 378 to 395, declared Christianity the official religion of Rome.

Under Constantine's favor, Christian communities grew steadily stronger and more numerous. Early Christians, contrary to common practice, recognized no concept of God other than their own, and no religious teachings other than the Word of Christ. The faith acquired an organizational structure in the second and third centuries that helped the religion thrive as an institution. At the center of the institution were the bishops, who were nominated by the other clergy. Each bishop controlled his own district, or diocese. Among the most important was the bishop of Rome, who claimed official descent from St. Peter, the first bishop of Rome and one of Jesus Christ's original apostles.

Dealing with Christian Heresies

Although Christianity had triumphed as a cultural force, Christian communities were torn by differences of opinion over doctrine and belief. Roman Catholicism, indeed, was only one of several forms of Christianity. A major element of the developing structure of the church was the official decisions that were made about what Christians truly believed. Groups who chose alternative versions were referred to, and condemned, as heretics.

The Council of Nicaea, called by Constantine in 325, officially condemned the largest of the Christian heresies, Arianism. Arius, a priest from Alexandria in Egypt, had argued that Jesus was fully human rather than divine. His bishop, Athanasius of Alexandria, claimed that Jesus was both God and man. The church leaders at Nicaea, siding with Athanasius, produced the Nicene Creed, stating as official church doctrine that God and Jesus shared the same "substance."

Another heresy, Monophysitism, supported a third alternative. Monophysites claimed that Jesus possessed a combination of human and divine qualities, but possessed only one true nature. Church leaders meeting again at the Council of Chalcedon in 451 decided that Jesus had a bipartite, or dual, nature, as both God and man, and the Monophysites were officially condemned.

While Western Christians continued to observe the Chalcedonian as well as the Nicaean views, the Eastern Church remained sympathetic to both Arians and Monophysites.

The Papacy Stakes its Claim

Dealing with heresies and issues of doctrine encouraged the development of a centralized church leadership. One such figure, the bishop of Rome, sought leadership of the entire Christian world. The Roman bishops claimed that their office automatically carried more authority than other bishoprics. The Gospel of Matthew in the New Testament had named the apostle Peter bishop of Rome, the greatest Christian messenger in the imperial capital. Peter had gone on to claim that the Christian church would be based in Rome. By the fifth century, and with the Roman Empire collapsing around them, Roman bishops had grown more aggressive in pursuing their claim to be descendants of Peter. They had begun answering to the name of "papa," or pope, as it was later translated into English.

Not all Christians, particularly those in the east, agreed that the Roman bishops had precedence over all others. The fall of the western Empire, however, as well as the growing separation between east and west, allowed the popes an opportunity to assert their authority. The first to do so decisively was Gregory I, pope from 590 to 604, also known as Gregory the Great. Gregory's great accomplishment was to

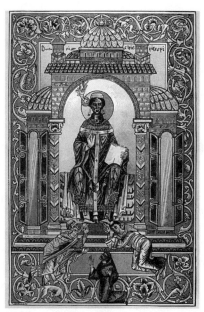

Pope Gregory I sends missionary monks to England to spread Christianity and to establish new monasteries.

turn the papacy into a political entity. He took control over a portion of central Italy later known as the Papal States, and governed the territory as if it were his own kingdom. Although he officially recognized the Byzantine emperor as the chief political figure in Christendom, Gregory realized that Constantinople was far away. The papacy therefore had to look after its own interests. Among the benefits of Gregory's political maneuver was that he gained further respect among the Germanic kings of early medieval Europe.

Gregory was also active in supporting the monastic movement. Aside from the papacy itself, the monastic movement was the most powerful tool of the church during the Early Middle Ages. Monks acted as missionaries to the unconverted. They founded schools and kept scholarship alive by storing and copying texts. The communities they lived in, monasteries, served not only religious and educational purposes but also became economic and administrative centers. In the Early Middle Ages, in fact, monasteries were the equivalent of towns.

Saint Benedict and the Monastic Movement

Originally, Christian monks in the west imitated their counterparts in the east. They separated themselves from society and tried to lead a simple life of self-denial, prayer, and devotion. Distance from the distractions and temptations of everyday life, they figured, would make it easier to keep their vows of chastity, poverty, and obedience.

In a Europe increasingly dominated by Roman Catholicism, however, monks began to gather into larger communities, which the church calls monastic orders, partly in self-defense. Germanic Europe could be violent and brutal. More important, however, was Christian leaders' conviction that monks should provide service to Christians and to the church, and that centralized monastic communities would better serve that purpose.

Credit for turning monasteries into centers of Christian activity goes largely to Benedict of Nursia. He founded the first Benedictine community at Monte Cassino in Italy in 529. Benedict's *Rule*, a pamphlet written sometime between

Benedict of Nursia meets with members of his order.

520 and 530, became the main guide for monastic activity. The *Rule* urged that monks lead an active, healthy life of service, rather than practicing solitude and self-denial. In addition to prayer and study, Benedict encouraged monks to perform physical labor, such as agricultural work. In fact, partly due to monastic labor, monasteries became centers of productive agriculture during the Early Middle Ages. They often produced more and better food than the feudal manors of the Germanic warlords.

Finally, Benedict helped enshrine another powerful office in the Roman Catholic hierarchy, and in so doing furthered the hold of the church on Western Europe. This was the abbot, the head of the monastery. The abbot's command over his monks, as well as any laypeople who might live and work in his monastery, was absolute. His opinion on all matters was decisive. Many abbots went on to serve roles as leaders in their territories. They were consulted not only on religious matters, but in legal disputes and economic crises as well.

While the Roman Catholic Church increased its influence in Western Europe, a different sort of Christianity emerged in the eastern portion of the old Roman Empire. In later eras this church would be called the Eastern Orthodox Church, and it would be based in Constantine's imperial capital, Constantinople.

The Hun Invasions and the Germanic Migrations

Instability in the Roman Empire had increased since Constantine's death in 337. His successors were unable to command the same respect, and the Romans, far from Constantinople, were unable to fend off attacks from the Germanic tribes; in any case, Rome's army itself was largely infiltrated by Germans. In addition, a new force, the Huns, had made the Germans even more volatile.

The Huns were nomadic peoples from central Asia who had organized themselves into large invading armies. Uninterested in conquest and settlement, the Huns sought plunder, and were among the most feared fighting forces of their day. Attracted by the wealth of the Roman Empire, wave after wave of Hun invasions beset Europe in the fourth and fifth centuries. In turn, the Hun invasions set off a series of migrations among the Germanic tribes, who sought to escape the Huns. These migrations wreaked havoc on Rome's European borders.

In the meantime, the split between the eastern and western parts of the empire was deepening. The emperor Valerian (364–375), realizing he could not defend both portions of the empire at the same time, appointed a coruler, his brother Valens. Valens was given control of the east, while

Valerian sought to maintain Rome's western possessions from his base in Milan in northern Italy. Both Valens and Valerian kept their own courts and administrations. Linguistic differences helped to cement the split. While Latin remained the major language of the west, Greek became the language of governance in the east.

In 376 the western Goths, or Visigoths, made arrangements to enter the eastern empire to help fight off the Huns. They later betrayed these arrangements. At the battle of Adrianople in 378, Valens was killed by his former Goth allies. His successor in Constantinople, Theodosius, sought to pacify the Goths rather than wreak revenge. He offered them leadership positions in his army and administration in addition to their share of the spoils of war. Theodosius, however, managed only to further weaken the empire, as Germanic peoples continued to flood across the now porous borders. Final insults came in the fifth century. In 410, a Visigoth army led by Alaric sacked Rome itself. In 452, the western emperor was forced to seek the help of the Goths to forestall an attack by Attila, king of the Huns.

The end of the western Roman Empire finally came in 476. In that year the final western emperor was overthrown by Odoacer, a barbarian warlord. Zeno, the eastern emperor at Constantinople, officially recognized Odoacer as the leader in the west. In turn, Odoacer proclaimed Zeno the sole Roman emperor. Western Europe now lay under the control of various Germanic kings.

The Byzantine Empire

Rome's imperial tradition, however, remained alive in the east, at Constantinople. The greatest of the early Byzantine emperors was Justinian, who ruled from 527 to 565. Byzantine rulers had long asserted their authority over Western Europe as well as Rome's former possessions in North Africa, and Justinian was no exception. In the 530s and 540s he sent his general, Belisarius, against the Germanic Vandals in North Africa and the Ostrogoths in Italy. Though the reconquest was ultimately successful, it came at a high cost. Much of Italy was devastated, not only by the fighting but by disease. The period was so ruinous, in fact, that it destroyed western Mediterranean economies for decades. And the Byzantine reconquest of the west was short; in 568 another Germanic tribe, the Lombards, invaded Italy and forced out much of the Byzantine army.

Justinian's greater legacy was his codification of Roman law. In support of his main political goal, which was to centralize all authority according to the policy of "one God, one empire, one religion," Justinian looked back to Rome at its height. He collected legal debates, imperial decrees, and scholarly commentary and organized his *Corpus Juris Civilis*, or *Body of Civil Law*. It was divided into four parts. First was the *Code*, which organized imperial decrees made since the second century. Next was the *New Laws*, which contained the edicts of Justinian and his successors. Thirdly, the *Digest* was a collection of commentary by scholars and lawyers. The fourth part was the *Institutes*, a guidebook for young legal scholars and administrators.

Justinian's codification of Roman law not only helped solidify the rule of the Byzantine emperors as well as the functions of their complicated bureaucracy, but served a broader historical purpose. It kept Roman law alive for rediscovery by western Europeans during the Renaissance of the fifteenth and sixteenth centuries.

Justinian's Building Program

Although Constantine had envisioned Constantinople as a major city from its inception, and Theodosius had placed it inside a network of walls, Justinian's building program made the Byzantine capital the Christian world's largest city and most important trade center during the Early Middle Ages. Justinian constructed a huge palace complex as well as a center of athletic competition known as the Hippodrome. To keep the people of the city occupied and orderly he put them to work on a number of grand public works projects, including roads, bridges, and huge underground reservoirs to supply the city with water.

The emperor was most interested, however, in building churches, and as head of the Eastern Christian Church, he

was in a position to order the construction of many. Of the numerous churches he built or reconstructed the greatest was the monumental Hagia Sophia in Constantinople. Hagia Sophia, indeed, became a symbol of the Byzantine Empire. It was constructed in such a way that the huge central dome appeared to be floating in space, and huge windows beneath the dome enhanced the entering light, giving the interior an always-changing quality; as Procopius, Justinian's court historian, pointed out, the light reminded people of God. Along with the palace and the Hippodrome, the dome of Hagia Sophia dominated the skyline of Constantinople.

Constantinople was the most populous city in Christendom during the Early Middle Ages, home to hundreds of thousands of people of a number of racial and linguistic backgrounds, although Greek was the main tongue. It also served as a trade center, a place where goods from all over the world were bought and sold. The capital's markets held spices from Asia, silk from China, and furs and amber from Russia. Naturally, the wealth and variety of available goods attracted visitors from all over the Old World of Europe, Africa, and Asia. Among the many visitors in the ninth and tenth centuries were Swedish Vikings who traveled via the Russian river system. They came seeking service as mercenaries to the emperor, as well as to trade.

The Emergence of Islam

By the early seventh century, the Byzantines were in need of military assistance: The greatest challenge to the Byzantine Empire, and to western Europe as well, was the new religion of Islam, which was spreading from its origin in Mecca, a crossroads city far to the south of Constantinople in Arabia. There, in about 610, a merchant by the name of Muhammad began to receive messages from the archangel Gabriel. Gabriel claimed that Muhammad was to be a prophet of God. The recitations of Gabriel were later compiled as the *Koran*, the Islamic holy book.

Convinced that he was, indeed, called to be a prophet of God (Allah in Arabic), Muhammad demanded that his fellow Arabs give up polytheism and the worship of idols. The people of Mecca refused, and forced him to flee. In 622, Muhammad formed the first true Islamic community in Medina, an Arabian city about 250 miles north of Mecca.

The followers of Islam, called Muslims, convinced they were called to spread their new faith, soon were transformed into a militant army. Led by Muhammad, the Muslims conquered Mecca in 624. Muhammad's successors, the caliphs, went on to conquer North Africa, the Persian Empire, and much of the modern Middle East, parts of which had been Byzantine territory. In the early eighth century, Islamic conquerors entered Western Europe, conquering Spain and threatening the Germanic kingdom of the Franks in modern France and Germany.

The new Islamic empire, centered first in Damascus and later in Baghdad, was to become a major center of trade, culture, and science. In addition, it was to be a constant threat to its Christian neighbors. The Islamic empire was at least the equal of the Byzantine Empire in wealth and power. As the Byzantine Empire focused on countering and controlling Muslim influence, western Europe further slipped from Byzantine authority.

The Germanic Kingdoms of Western Europe

The Germanic presence in the Roman Empire had been expanding for centuries. The various Germanic peoples of Europe, called barbarians by the more urbanized, civilized Romans, were little more than small, semicivilized, nomadic tribes when the Romans first encountered them in the second and first centuries B.C. During the Pax Romana of the first two hundred years after the birth of Jesus Christ, many Germans had simply been brought into Rome as servants or soldiers. Others continued to live a nomadic lifestyle in Roman Gaul, a region which encompassed much of modern France and Germany.

The Germanic tribes that ultimately established control over Britain were the Angles and Saxons, who were migrants from Scandinavia. Up to seven Anglo-Saxon kingdoms co-existed at various times, but all had a great deal in common, in particular the same language. The common Anglo-Saxon tongue made it easier for the kingdoms to be converted to Roman Catholic Christianity in the 700s and 800s.

Ultimately the greatest of the Germanic kingdoms was that established by the Franks, who inhabited much of Roman Gaul. Once they were united under King Clovis (481–511), the Franks became a powerful force, quickly establishing dominance over the Romanized inhabitants of the region. Adding to Clovis's influence was the fact that he converted to Roman Catholic Christianity rather than Arianism, as many of the other German kings had done. His conversion to Roman Catholicism ensured that he would have the support of the papacy and church hierarchy. In addition, the Franks could now claim to be the true defenders of the Christian faith, and use the claim as an excuse for military aggression.

Clovis's kingdom also paved the way for a new culture, which combined Roman traditions with Germanic ways. This Roman-Frankish combination was to be the driving force, in fact, behind the emergence of a distinctly western European culture. Germanic officials in the larger towns, for instance, shared authority with Roman bishops, combining what remained of Roman law with Germanic customary law. In addition, Frankish and Roman elites frequently intermarried, which ultimately produced a new ruling class.

The widespread Frankish kingdom, despite its unifying

ties to Catholic authorities, was frequently beset by conflicts among the powerful Frankish ruling families. Clovis had established the Merovingian dynasty, which was to be the most important of these families until the eighth century. Other families, however, demanded autonomy in their own regions, and frequently the Frankish kingdom was divided into smaller parts such as, by 700, Austrasia in the east, Neustria in northern Gaul, and the southern kingdom of Burgundy.

Germanic Society

Germanic society, up to and even beyond the eighth century, was still largely organized into small, rival tribes, although certain groups, like the Frankish elites, had begun to grow less fractured. Societies were organized around their warlord kings, who claimed that they were descended from the gods. Even after the Germans converted to Christianity, which was often only a matter of the king's conversion (his people followed automatically), kings claimed to possess the divine authority of the Christian God. To be a king, however, could be a heavy responsibility; Germanic kings were held personally responsible for the welfare of their peoples.

The basic social unit in Germanic society was the extended family, and kinship ties were more important than any other. The extended family was the source of sustenance and protection, and one could expect to call on his kinfolk in times of trouble or crisis. Land was passed down within the family, families worked together in the fields, and, indeed, fathers, brothers, sons, and uncles fought together on the battlefield.

The Germanic armies brought together numerous kinship groups, which gave Germanic society a militaristic tone. Indeed, warfare was epidemic in Germanic Europe, and life could be brutal overall. For example, if a person's word could not be deemed true or false, he or she might be subjected to an ordeal that was supposed to reveal God's verdict. Such ordeals included having a hand plunged into boiling water, or being bound by rope and then thrown into a pond. If the person concerned floated, it meant that God approved of him or her. Sinking meant that God had made the opposite judgment.

Women in Germanic society had very few legal rights. They were at birth the property of their fathers, and upon marriage the property of their husbands. The only women who could legally own property were widows. Often, however, women carried a high legal value, or "wergeld." Wergeld was what the Germanic peoples felt was the monetary equivalent of a human being. The system developed as an alternative to military vengeance; if someone killed or injured an enemy, he might simply be required to pay wergeld to the victim's family. Women of childbearing age, for their part, had a particularly high wergeld due to their value to their families and tribes.

The Carolingians

In the early eighth century, Merovingian kings still controlled the Frankish lands, but they were challenged by a family known as the Carolingians. The Carolingians had come to control an office known as mayor of the palace. The office, officially simply that of a court spokesman, was the true power in the Frankish territories. The mayor of the palace had the opportunity, among other rights, to grant land, known as benefices or fiefs, to powerful nobles. Charles Martel, the head of the Carolingians from 714 until 741, took advantage of this privilege to create a huge mounted army. These knights, having been granted fiefs by Charles Martel, were obligated to support him in war as well as in politics.

Charles Martel's reputation as the true leader of the Franks was cemented in 732. In that year his army defeated an invading Islamic army at Poitiers in modern France. This checked the Arab advance into western Europe, thus ensuring that the Arab Muslims would remain confined to Spain while northwestern Europe remained Roman Catholic.

The Carolingians, however, could not claim the kingship of the Franks. Only members of the Merovingian clan could be kings, at least until the papacy had ordained a change. The obvious solution was a formal agreement between the Carolingians and the pope to switch the Frankish kingship to the Carolingians. Charles Martel, however, refused any such offer on the part of the pope, fearing limits to his true authority.

An agreement was finally reached between Charles Martel's son, Pepin III (741–768) and Pope Zacharias (741–752). Zacharias removed the last Merovingian ruler and established the Carolingian kingship of the Franks. In return, he expected military support, when necessary, from the Carolingians. Pepin III was duly named king in 751. Only two years later, a new pope, Stephen (752–757) demanded Pepin's help against the Lombards. By 754 the alliance between king and pope had been sealed. The Franks were acknowledged as the true defenders of the western Christian Church, not only against the Lombards but against the Byzantine Empire and the Muslims as well. Pepin also recognized Pope Stephen's role as a territorial leader by granting him control over a stretch of territory in central Italy later known as the Papal States.

Pepin III is proclaimed king in 751 with the support of Pope Zacharias.

Despite the alliance between Pepin III and Zacharias, a continual struggle for authority between popes and kings existed throughout the Middle Ages. In the early stages of the controversy a document appeared that was designed to defend the claims of the popes. This document was the so-called Donation of Constantine, which claimed that Constantine had declared that the papacy and the Roman Catholic Church were the true heirs to the Roman Empire. The church's authority extended not only to religious matters but to political and territorial disputes as well, according to the document. In the fifteenth century the Donation of Constantine was proved to be a fraud. Nonetheless, it was accepted as true in the Carolingian era, and it indicates the lengths to which the church was willing to go to defend itself against the growing power of the Carolingian kings.

Charlemagne and the Holy Roman Empire

The greatest of the Carolingians was Pepin's son, Charlemagne. His accomplishments were many. Between 768, the year he took the throne, and his death in 814, Frankish territory expanded to include modern France, Holland, Belgium, Switzerland, and most of Germany and Italy. In addition, Charlemagne established new ties with the Byzantine Empire and stabilized western European borders against both the Muslims and a new group of Hun invaders known as the Avars.

Charlemagne had greater ambitions, however; he wanted to rule an empire. To give himself the proper stage he constructed a new imperial capital at Aachen in Germany, modeled after Byzantium. He also considered himself the head of the Roman Catholic Church, just as the Byzantine emperor was the leader of the Eastern Church. Finally, on Christmas Day 800, Charlemagne was able to fulfill his imperial ambitions; Pope Leo III crowned him Holy Roman Emperor.

In this Charlemagne was able to take advantage of unique circumstances. The throne in Constantinople was vacant for a brief period due to a question over who had the legitimate claim to be emperor. One of the claimants was the empress Irene, who blinded her son, the rightful heir, in order to assume power. Few leaders in east or west, in any case, accepted Irene's claim because she was a woman. The vacancy in Constantinople meant that no one, at that moment, held

Emperor Charlemagne revived formal learning during his reign offering money and land to scholars who would come to his court.

the title of Roman emperor. Charlemagne sought to step into the breach.

For his part, Pope Leo III sought protection against enemies in Rome, who had little faith in him as the head of the church. This protection was to come from Charlemagne, who, in return for guaranteeing Leo's papacy, demanded the imperial throne. The arrangement benefited both king and pope.

The Holy Roman Empire, this alliance of convenience between Charlemagne and Leo, was intended, again, to be a revival of the earlier Roman Empire in the west. In addition, it was to serve as a balance to the power of the Byzantines as well as the Arab empire at Baghdad. Both eastern emperors, Byzantine and Arab, respected Charlemagne and recognized his authority as emperor of the west. In fact, the Arab caliph, Harun al-Rashid, sent Charlemagne a white elephant as a token of his goodwill.

Charlemagne's reign also featured the first attempt in western Europe to revive classical and formal learning, known as the Carolingian Renaissance. Charlemagne was interested in creating a new and loyal generation of churchmen and administrators, and he was willing to spend the money necessary to fulfill this goal. He offered scholars, many of whom came from monasteries in the British Isles, money and grants of land if they came to his court at Aachen. Such scholars as Alcuin of York taught Greek, Roman, and Christian studies in the new schools.

Administrators studied subjects that would help them in their tasks. The basic curriculum was made up of what the scholars of the day considered the seven liberal arts: grammar, dialectic, logic, arithmetic, geometry, astronomy, and music. Administrators were thus trained in such basic skills as oration, reasoning, and calculating.

Charlemagne's scholars also worked to preserve old texts and increase literacy. One of their major projects was to provide an accurate, accessible Latin translation of the Bible as well as the works of other early Christian thinkers. Their efforts helped to create a simple, uniform, scholarly Latin, which was to be the basic language of western Europe's intellectual life for centuries.

As always, Charlemagne's goals were not merely cultural and educational, although he certainly valued education for its own sake. He wanted to form a loyal, uniformly trained bureaucracy. The government of the Holy Roman Empire was carried out through a dual system of counts and special royal officers known as *missi dominici*. The system of counts dated back to Merovingian times. Counts were powerful, landowning Germanic nobles who were expected to provide their king with military support. In addition, they were expected to collect taxes and administer the king's laws.

To prevent the counts from growing too independent within their domains, Charlemagne's *missi dominici* reinforced Charlemagne's policies. These officials were both clerical and lay administrators who made annual visits to regions away from their homes. As such, the missi dominici represent another example of Charlemagne's reasonably successful combination of church and state.

Charlemagne's death resulted, ultimately, in a breakup of the Holy Roman Empire. It proved too large and unwieldy for central control; and despite the efforts of Charlemagne's special agents, local counts sought independence from Carolingian restrictions. In addition, Charlemagne's grandsons sought their own kingdoms, which was in accordance with Frankish custom if not the larger interests of the Holy Roman Emperor. An agreement signed by the three grandsons in 843, the Treaty of Verdun, replaced the empire with three independent states, whose conflicts would play major roles in European history into the twentieth century. The three kingdoms corresponded roughly to France in the west, Germany in the east, and an unsettled area between the two.

Charlemagne's empire, nonetheless, had helped revive the possibility of western European dominance. In addition, Roman Catholic Christianity established its place at the center of European civilization when Charlemagne, as emperor, pledged to defend the Roman Catholic Church.

Lords and Vassals

During the era of Carolingian domination, the medieval political-economic system known as feudalism developed and expanded. Ultimately, feudalism provided western Europe with a marginally coherent social order in the Early Middle Ages.

Feudalism was based on the domination of society by landowning warlords. During the Early Middle Ages, warfare among these warlords was chronic, and alliances were forged as weaker lords sought protection and stronger lords sought support. In addition, the common people required protection and sustenance in a world constantly destabilized by warfare.

The system began to develop in Merovingian France,

when certain free warriors began to ally themselves with stronger counterparts. Those who looked for protection, the weaker warriors, came to be known as vassals, which means "those who serve." The more powerful princes, for their part, saw this as an opportunity to not only build larger armies but expand their lands.

By Carolingian times, many princes were actively seeking to acquire new vassals, and the number of vassals a lord could command was the main measure of his power and authority. Because princes could rarely support all of their vassals materially, they began, instead, to award them grants of land. These grants were known as benefices or fiefs. Any vassal who accepted a fief from his lord was bound, in gratitude, to serve him at war and at court. Also, vassals were expected to govern their fiefs.

Another element of the arrangements between lords and vassals was the performance of homage, or fealty. Fealty could take many forms. Military service was the most basic, but others include the performance of ceremonies of subservience, such as the kissing of a lord's ring. Alternatively, a vassal might be required to lend his lord money, if necessary, or work for him on his estate. Fealty also carried tones of religious devotion; in swearing fealty to his lord, a vassal was pledging before God to remain loyal to his lord.

Bishops and abbots also became part of the feudal structure in the ninth and tenth centuries. Late Carolingian kings forced these religious leaders to swear fealty to them. The fiefs they received in return were their church offices as well as grants of land. The church would later oppose the right of kings to choose bishops and abbots in this manner as inappropriately putting spiritual power in the hands of secular kings. The conflict between the church and kings over such matters was to be a constant theme of the later Middle Ages.

Feudal Serfs

Most Europeans, however, were neither lord nor vassal nor high churchman. The majority of the population were agricultural peasants. In the feudal era these peasants were divided into two groups: free and unfree serfs. Free serfs were peasants who had owned their land, yet gave it up to a feudal landlord in exchange for protection. The land was then, generally, leased back to the free serf to use as he liked, provided he performed services for his lord. Such services might include labor in the manorial household or support on the battlefield. In addition, a free serf might have to give up a certain percentage of his crop every year.

Unfree serfs were peasants with little property to offer any lord in exchange for his protection. They might have nothing to offer beyond a few farming implements, or their own backs. The demands lords made on them were, consequently, much higher. Unfree serfs might have to work on the lord's lands three days out of the week. They might have to give up more than half of their crop for the lord's use. They were unfree, moreover, because they were bound to their manors by ties of debt, obligation, or fealty. While such serfs were not slaves in that they were never bought or sold as human beings, they were not free to leave their lands and their lords. They were forced to pay rent, and were subject to their lords' judgment in any dispute. The only breaks that unfree serfs ever enjoyed from a life of constant toil were infrequent religious holidays, which sometimes also served as market days.

The feudal manor was the basic social and economic unit of the era. It was divided into several portions. The land maintained for the lord himself often made up one-quarter to one-third of the property. It was called the demesne and contained, of course, the manorial household, which in the Early Middle Ages was a simple structure of stonework rather than a castle. The remainder of the manor consisted of land leased to free and unfree serfs, who were provided with simple shacks to live in, and the common grounds, which were generally given over to grazing livestock.

New Invasions

Between approximately 780 and 1050, western Europeans were the targets of another series of violent invasions. The upheaval caused by these invasions created a number of problems ranging from devastated cities and monasteries to uprooted populations to destroyed agricultural lands. In the aftermath of the invasions, however, Europeans grew more creative and innovative. Improvements in agriculture yielded more food. Migratory populations cleared new agricultural lands. In addition, the rigid feudal structure that had emerged during Carolingian times was challenged, resulting in greater opportunities for more people.

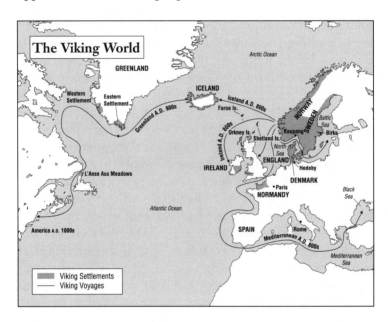

The invasions themselves came from three directions. From the south came a new Muslim onslaught, which was primarily directed at Italy. For a brief period Muslims conquered Sicily and southern Italy, turning most of the Mediterranean into a Muslim lake. From the east came yet another Hun invasion. In this case the Huns were known as Magyars. After a few decades of violence and plunder, the Magyars settled down in the plain of the Danube River in central Europe. There they converted to Roman Catholicism and, ultimately, created the kingdom of Hungary.

The worst of the invasions, as far as western Europeans were concerned, came from the north. These were the invasions of the Norsemen, or Vikings. Their plundering raids constituted the final Germanic migration into western Europe. Like their earlier counterparts, the Vikings eventually settled down, converted to Christianity, and established more stable kingdoms.

The Viking invasions, however, were a shock to European society. The first raids took place in the late eighth century, the result, probably, of overpopulation and starvation in the Vikings' Scandinavian homelands. In this instance the Vikings attacked monasteries and settlements in the British Isles, inspiring fear throughout Europe with stories of their brutality. In the ninth and tenth centuries, however, many Norwegian and Danish Vikings settled permanently in the British Isles, where they mixed with the local populations. Some of the early English kings, in fact, were descendants of these Norsemen. During the ninth century the Vikings also attacked the Frankish territories on the European continent. Their prowess as sailors and warriors made them formidable enemies, and Frankish defenses were not always adequate. Often instead the Franks tried to buy off the Vikings with grants of land or with money. Normandy, a province of northern France, is just one example. The first duke of Normandy, Rollo, was a Norseman (or Norman). He was granted the territory by Louis the Pious, Charlemagne's grandson. From Normandy, England was successfully invaded in 1066 by William the Conqueror. William himself, as well as his army, was of Viking descent.

Other groups of Vikings ranged even farther afield. Some went into the Mediterranean, to Spain and Italy, where they battled the Muslims. Norwegian Vikings crossed the North Atlantic, settling Iceland, Greenland, and for a short time, a colony in North America they called Vinland. Swedish Vikings, seeking trade and plunder rather than conquest, traveled to the east. They moved down the Russian rivers and made their way to Constantinople. There were a number of instances of Swedish Vikings, whom the Byzantines called "Rus" because of their reddish hair, serving as mercenaries in the emperor's army.

The Vikings integrated themselves rather easily into the feudal structure at first. By the year 1000, however, the system had grown complex and unwieldy. Many vassals, for instance, had vassals of their own. It was also common for vassals to have fealty arrangements with more than one lord, and some had manorial landholdings that were separated by hundreds of miles. Another problem was that church officials, despite their oaths of fealty, sought independence from feudal landlords on religious grounds.

The feudal system began to break down after 1000, as western Europe began to revive economically and culturally. New agricultural techniques, such as the use of the heavy plow, improved the food supply, which in turn allowed the population to grow. In addition, trade with the east expanded, creating another source of wealth. Some feudal nobles turned to trade rather than warfare. The expansion of trade, in its turn, revived urban life. Towns were a major challenge to feudalism, as in the Early Middle Ages towns were considered to be free places. Many serfs ran away to towns, where they could work and live as free men. Towns also became centers of learning, culture, and commerce.

Many aspects of feudal Europe remained in place. Kings still commanded their vassals and warfare was a constant threat. But western Europe had begun to move into a new era: the High Middle Ages. It was able to do so on a reasonably secure foundation. This foundation was the combination of Roman culture, Germanic traditions, and Catholic Christianity that had developed during the Early Middle Ages.

Chapter 1

The Early Roman Catholic Church

Turning | Points
IN WORLD HISTORY

The Roman Catholic Church Takes Shape

H.G. Koenigsberger

Christianity had spread widely throughout Europe by the time the Roman Empire began to break apart in the third and fourth centuries. As the empire declined, more people turned to the new religion as a source of stability and comfort. In addition, as H.G. Koenigsberger suggests in this excerpt from his history of Europe during the Middle Ages, Christianity also gained authority because it was able to absorb ideas from earlier periods of Greek and Roman history. An example of this integration was the work of the early Christian thinker St. Augustine.

Koenigsberger adds, however, that early Christianity was challenged by a variety of interpretations of Church doctrine. Early religious leaders considered these challenges to be heresies. The two largest heresies were Arianism and Monophysitism. Arians argued that Jesus Christ was human rather than divine. Monophysites believed that Christ was fully divine while he was on earth. Both heresies had important political followers, which made them difficult for the Church to attack openly.

Disputes such as those over heresy inevitably led to the involvement of the Roman emperors in religious debates. Finally, with the support of the emperors, the Christian church in western Europe rejected the important heresies, and established a secure system of belief, or doctrine. The western church was to be a catholic, or universal, church, and it was to be based on the idea that Jesus Christ was both human and god.

H.G. Koenigsberger is professor of history at King's College, London.

Excerpted from H.G. Koenigsberger, *Medieval Europe: 400–1500.* Copyright © 1987 H.G. Koenigsberger. Reprinted with permission from Longman Group UK Ltd.

By the year 400 Christianity had become the predominant religion of the Roman world. There were good reasons for this success. In the first place, there was the powerful appeal of a belief which promised eternal life and spiritual peace to all men regardless of their present condition. For life on earth was hard, painful and short for most people; and as if this were not comfortless enough, they also believed themselves beset by evil forces, demons who, it was thought, practised their malicious crafts on people's possessions, on their health and even on their sanity. Such age-old popular beliefs had been strengthened by the direct or indirect influence on the Roman intelligentsia of Persian Zoroastrianism, with its view of the universe as a battlefield between the independent forces of good and evil. The Christian theologians argued fiercely about the origins of evil; but they did not deny the existence and power of the demons. Indeed, they defined the ancient Greek and Roman gods as demons. But they also claimed—and this was their trump card—that through the grace of Jesus Christ they had power to do battle with the demons and to overcome them.

The Roman Emperor Constantine Turns to Christianity

The counterpart of the victory of Christ's spiritual soldiers, the monks, hermits and holy men, over His spiritual enemies was the victory of Christ's military soldiers over His earthly enemies. Since Constantine's victory over a rival emperor at the Milvian Bridge (A.D. 312) which assured his succession to the Empire and which he ascribed to the Christian God, the military power of the cross came to be accepted with increasing conviction. Old-fashioned pagans protested that the military disasters of the time were signs of the displeasure of the ancient gods at their recent neglect. They were drowned out by the chorus of Christian moralists who, to the contrary, saw these disasters as God's punishment for an insufficiently Christianized world.

Some Christians took a more profound view. St Augustine, bishop of Hippo in Africa, had arrived at his Christian beliefs by way of a long spiritual and intellectual struggle. In his *Confessions* he has left us an account of this struggle. From this personal and spiritual autobiography we know more about the sensibilities of the age, the blending of religious and philosophical thinking, than from any other early Christian source. 'I believe that I may understand,' was St Augustine's own summing up of his position. His penetrating self-perception, including the perception of his own sexuality, was to become a model for later autobiographical writers, up to our own time.

The sack of Rome by the Visigoths, in 410, left St Augustine as dismayed as most of his contemporaries. His famous book, *The City of God*, was, however, less a reaction to this apparently apocalyptic event than a fundamental attack on the still surviving paganism and a summary and final conclusion to his own thinking about the relation between heaven and earth. The glory of Rome, as it was traditionally seen by both pagans and Christians, was irrelevant to the glory which could be achieved only in the City of God. This was Jerusalem, the spiritual city of all true Christians, both alive and dead, and of God's angels. As against Jerusalem, Babylon was the city of this world. The earthly city which does not live by faith seeks an earthly peace, and the end it proposes in the well-ordered concord of civic obedience and rule, is the combination of men's wills to attain the things which are helpful to this life. The heavenly city, or rather the part of it which sojourns on earth and lives by faith, makes use of this peace only because it must, until 'this mortal condition which necessitates it shall pass away'. In this world the two cities were mixed together, but at the Last Judgement they would be separated.

The profundities and subtleties of Augustine's thought were to nourish a thousand years of Catholic and, eventually, also of Protestant theology. But for political ideas the basic concept came to be Augustine's acknowledgement that worldly, political government and authority were useful, or even necessary, for the pursuit of a Christian life here on earth. In practice this teaching meant a further strengthening of the tradition by which the Christian Church, ever since it had accepted the special favours bestowed on it by the emperor Constantine, had supported secular political authority. With only a few exceptions, the Catholic Church has since remained on the side of established authority; but it could question, and often has questioned, what was legitimate authority.

Christianity Was Combined with Earlier Ideas

There was one further element in the development of Christianity which was absolutely necessary for its victory. This was its acceptance and assimilation of the intellectual traditions of the pre-Christian Roman world. Without such an acceptance it is difficult to believe that Christianity would not have simply remained one of the mystery cults of which there were a great number in the Roman Empire. There were those in the early Church who wanted to reject all Roman culture as pagan. They remained in a minority. It simply proved impossible to divorce serious theological thought from the existing traditions and systems of education. From at least as early as the beginning of the third century the great theologians were also learned men, deliberately harnessing pagan rhetoric, science and philosophy to the purposes of Christian thinking and education.

It was not always easy to do this with a good conscience; for was there not vanity in the pursuit of classical learning? St Augustine again shows the conflicts in Christian learning during this period; but characteristically he attempts to overcome these conflicts. Augustine accepted the Neo-Platonists' concept of plenitude, the fullness of the world of all possible types of creation (for God was bound to have created everything that could have been created; otherwise one would have had to suppose that there were limits to God's goodness and creativeness, which was inconceivable). Having accepted this, Augustine also accepted the argument that therefore there must exist an infinite scale of beings, from the angels down to the lowliest worm and to inanimate things. This was the theory of 'the great chain of being'. It was to remain a basic concept in western philosophy and theology until at least the Romantic period of the nineteenth century. In the fifth century, it enabled Augustine to accept the value of classical learning while at the same time severely subordinating it to the higher, religious aims which man should pursue.

Not all Christians managed to handle this problem as tidily as the great St Augustine. Justinian expelled the pagan teachers from the academy of Athens and thus effectively broke a thousand-year tradition of Greek philosophy. But on the whole, the Church, without ever entirely losing its ambivalent feelings about secular culture, came to be the guardian and preserver of the Greek and Roman pagan traditions. Often it was a selective, even capricious guardianship. But the fact of preservation itself was to be of enormous importance to Europe; for it provided a vision of a golden world, glimpsed indeed only from tantalizing fragments, but admired and even venerated, a perennial spur to imitation and emulation. Time and again, during the next thousand years, this vision was to inspire the most creative cultural efforts of European society. The philosophical traditions introduced by St Augustine and other Church fathers into Christianity made necessary at least a certain degree of acceptance of this world. Spirit and flesh, heaven and earth, would war with each other but never be completely separated in the western Christian tradition. It proved to be an uncomfortable but a fruitful heritage.

The Heresies That Challenged Early Christianity

Given the nature of Christian beliefs and the reasons for its spread in the Roman Empire, it is not surprising that it should have been beset by heresies. If personal salvation depended on a specific belief, and if God was to help the believer against both his mortal and his spiritual enemies, then it seemed clear that he had to get his beliefs absolutely right. This conviction would apply at all intellectual levels, from the philosophically trained theologian, worrying about the nature of the Trinity, to the most simple and illiterate peasant praying for divine help against the natural and demonic forces that were constantly threatening him. But what was correct belief? Scripture could be interpreted in different ways—and was by the theologians of the period.

In the eastern part of the Roman Empire, their differ-

Religious beliefs varied greatly throughout the Roman Empire.

ences centred on the nature of Christ and the precise nature of his relation to God. If the theologians' arguments were often difficult to understand they were still a matter of the utmost importance to every individual; for on the precise nature of Christ must surely depend one's own salvation. But while the origins of such differing beliefs and even much of their popular appeal were strictly theological, they always became entangled with other, more worldly motivations. The Goths and Vandals accepted the doctrine of the Egyptian Arius, a belief that Christ was not fully equal with God the Father. No doubt, they believed themselves to be theologically correct; but equally they seem to have clung to a doctrine declared heretical by a Roman church council in order to emphasize their difference from the Romans. Armenians, Syrians and Egyptians wanted as much to emphasize their cultural differences from the Greeks as insist on different theological beliefs when they adopted Nestorianism (belief in the basically human nature of Christ) or Monophysitism (belief in Christ's purely divine nature).

The quarrels of the theologians, mixed up as they were with the disputes of the patriarchs of Constantinople, Antioch, Alexandria and of the pope of Rome over pre-eminence in the Christian Church and reinforced by the local loyalties of the urban mobs of the great eastern cities, became a more and more intractable problem for the emperors. In Egypt and Syria the Monophysites predominated. They had allies or sympathizers in the capital, among the 'greens' of the circus parties and right up to the court and even to Justinian's empress, Theodora. But the great majority of the Greeks, together with the popes and the westerners, were orthodox, holding fast to the doctrine laid down by the council of Chalcedon in 451, that Christ had a dual nature, both divine and human. The emperors manoeuvred between the parties, generally favouring the orthodox, but unwilling to crush the Monophysites completely, for fear of losing Syria and Egypt. They had good grounds for such a fear. The religious tensions between these provinces and Constantinople at least help to explain their unwillingness to defend themselves against the Arabs in the seventh century.

In the west where the theological conflicts centred on the relation between God and man, rather than on the nature of Christ, there was a similar confusion of religious and secular motivation. The most immediately serious schism, or split, in the western Church was the Donatist movement. It had arisen out of a quarrel over the behaviour of African bishops during the persecutions of Diocletian and had effectively led to the establishment of a separatist African Church which could call for support on regional loyalties and social discontent. Its doctrinal differences from orthodox doctrine were slight; but it was one of St Augustine's major problems and it was not fully resolved until the Vandal conquest of Africa. . . .

Since Christianity had won its great victories through the support of the state, it was inevitable that the Church should involve the state in its religious controversies. The head of the Christian community in each city was the bishop, and it was the bishops who assembled in council and determined matters of doctrine. But it was the emperor who, from the time of Constantine, summoned the councils of the whole Church (ecumenical councils), and it was at his insistence and by his authority that orthodox doctrine was defined and imposed. The first ecumenical council, that of Nicaea (325), condemned Arius and defined the doctrine of the Trinity. The fourth, the council of Chalcedon (451), condemned Nestorius and the Monophysites and confirmed the doctrine of the two distinct natures of Christ, the divine and the human. In the east the emperor never lost his power over the councils and over the declaration of Christian doctrine. The Church, in so far as it remained orthodox, also remained effectively subordinate to his authority. When the Monophysite bishops of Egypt and Syria repudiated the orthodoxy established by virtue of imperial authority, they did not perhaps immediately see that this involved also a political repudiation of the emperor. By the seventh century, however, this too had become clear.

The Pope's Authority Was Political as Well as Religious

Richard Barber

The Roman Catholic Church, in effect, replaced the Roman Empire in western Europe after the fall of the western Empire in the fifth century. The Church had all the trappings of a government, including law courts and tax collectors. Perhaps more importantly, the Church was headed by the Bishop of Rome, known more informally as *papa* or pope. During the Early Middle Ages, the papacy operated much like a kingdom.

In this selection from his history of medieval Europe, Richard Barber describes how the Church adopted administrative practices and even religious sites from Rome. During the sixth century, after the Roman Empire had been dismembered by various invaders, the pope became in reality the temporal, or political, leader of Rome, and the most important political figure in western Europe.

Barber notes, however, that the pope's political authority was frequently challenged. At first the greatest challenges came from the emperor of the surviving eastern, or Byzantine, empire. Later, the pope found himself limited by Germanic kings such as Pepin III, king of the Franks in the mid-700s. Nonetheless, the Church remained the main source of earthly stability throughout the Early Middle Ages.

Richard Barber is a founder of the publishing firm Boydell and Brewer, Limited, and is the author of a number of books on the Middle Ages.

It was Christianity that gave medieval Europe its identity and unity: from Iceland to Sicily, from Portugal to Finland, you could go into a church and attend a service in which the rit-

Excerpted from Richard Barber, *The Penguin Guide to Medieval Europe*. Copyright © 1984 Richard Barber. Reprinted with permission from the author.

ual and the language were largely the same. The organization of the church was correspondingly vast, an international bureaucracy which ran parallel to the secular government, with its own revenues and courts. It was hardly surprising if the spiritual world seemed remote from the everyday preoccupations of many of the clergy, and yet the church's authority was never seriously challenged during these centuries.

This vast network of power had grown up gradually and often by chance. Although Christianity had become the official religion of the Roman empire only under Theodosius I in 391, it was Christianity that came into much of the inheritance of the emperors. By the end of the fifth century, when the western empire was beginning to crumble before the barbarian onslaughts, Christianity was firmly established throughout Gaul, Spain and Italy; it was perhaps less secure in Britain, where there were some signs of a reversion to paganism. When the secular imperial administration collapsed, its shadow, the church hierarchy, often survived, preserving the old patterns and eventually providing the base for a renewal of government under the barbarian kings. For instance, in Gaul the bishoprics were based on the old Roman centres of administration, the cities; and although there are exceptions—two or three Roman *civitates* [cities] which did not become bishoprics, and half a dozen bishoprics centred on towns which had never been cities—the church continued the imperial pattern. Many medieval cathedrals are built on the site of great pagan temples; to take only two examples, the cathedral of Lectoure in south-west France was built on the place where a temple dedicated to Cybele had once stood, whose worshippers were initiated by being drenched in the blood of a slaughtered bull; at Uppsala in Sweden, the temple sacred to the Norse gods, with its grove where nine male victims of every species were sacrificed every ninth year, became the site of the archbishop's cathedral in the eleventh century.

The Bishop of Rome, the Pope, Becomes the Head of the Western Church

At the centre, in Rome itself, the head of the church inherited imperial titles and ambitions. The pre-eminence of the bishop of Rome as father (*Papa*) of the church was largely brought about by the emperors. Rome, it is true, was the oldest bishopric in the west, tracing its origins back to St Peter. But other apostles had founded other sees in the east, which were of equal seniority: Antioch, which also claimed St Peter as its founder, and Alexandria, which was said to have been founded by Mark. Other churches with less wealth and authority could also lay claim to apostolic foundation: Corinth, Ephesus, Thessalonika, Smyrna, Philippi. But these were not politically influential. As early as the beginning of the third century A.D., pope Calixtus I invoked the words of Our Lord to St Peter—'on this rock I will build my church'—and tried to assert his authority over other churches. His efforts were in vain, and the church remained loosely organized, as a union of independent bodies, during the years of persecution which preceded the first edict of tolerance under Constantine in the early fourth century. Constantine, although he was baptized only on his death-bed and never made his personal position as a Christian clear until that moment, favoured the church and gave freely to it, as did his mother Helena. It was he who gave the Lateran Palace to the bishops of Rome as their official residence, and built the first church in Rome there, using as model the classical public building known as a basilica, a spacious hall with a wooden roof. His dealings with the church seem to have been part of a scheme to use it as a state religion which would bind together the empire: he interfered in matters of purely spiritual importance, condemning one heresy personally at a church council in 316 and attempting to resolve another by his own compromise formula in 325. Constantine wanted a unified church, obedient to the emperor. As part of that policy, he promoted the bishop of Rome's claim to be *Papa* or pope, final arbiter of disputes and ruler of a single church. For Constantine must at least be credited with political foresight: much of the turmoil of the later Roman empire was occasioned by violent theological controversy, over points of belief which were sometimes central and crucial, sometimes unbelievably obscure. These theological controversies spilled over into secular life: the Arian heresy, which

Constantine tried to resolve in 325, almost gave rise to a separate and parallel church, at its zenith holding sway in Spain, north Africa and much of Italy, determining the allegiances of kings. Hence a spiritual authority was needed to ensure political harmony.

Pope Gregory the Great Was the Equal of Christ's Original Apostles

In his Ecclesiastical History, *written in the early eighth century, the English monk Bede (the "venerable") acknowledged the importance of Pope Gregory I as the leader of all Christians.*

At this time, that is, in the year of our Lord 605, the blessed Pope Gregory, after having most gloriously governed the Roman apostolic see thirteen years, six months, and ten days, died, and was translated to the eternal see of the heavenly kingdom. Of whom, in regard that he by his zeal converted our nation, the English, from the power of Satan to the faith of Christ, it behoves us to discourse more at large in our Ecclesiastical History, for we may and ought rightly to call him our apostle; because, whereas he bore the pontifical power over all the world, and was placed over the churches already reduced to the faith of truth, he made our nation, till then given up to idols, the church of Christ, so that we may be allowed thus to attribute to him the character of an apostle; for though he is not an apostle to others, yet he is so to us; for we are the seal of his apostleship in our Lord.

Selection from Bede, *Ecclesiastical History*, reprinted in *The Early Middle Ages: 500–1000*, ed. Robert Brentano. New York: Macmillan/Free Press, 1964.

But Rome was not necessarily the place for that authority. The imperial capital was at Milan from 286 until 402, and the bishopric of that city, particularly under St Ambrose, enjoyed great influence. Constantinople became co-capital in 330, and the empire was formally divided in two halves in 395. In 402 the western capital was moved to Ravenna; in 410 the Goths sacked Rome. Rome, in the early fifth century, was therefore only a provincial city in the western empire. Furthermore, the emperors were trying to make Constantinople a see second only to Rome, and it was the appearance of this dangerous rival that spurred the bishops of Rome into their formal claim for control of the whole church. Their moment of opportunity came under Leo I, in the mid fifth century. With the west in chaos and the east divided by heresies, he boldly claimed the primacy, and the emperor Valentinian III decreed, in 455, that if 'any bishop summoned to trial before the bishop of Rome shall neglect to come', the imperial authorities—such as they were—were to compel him to come. Leo also succeeded in getting his views on church doctrine accepted by the council of Chalcedon in Asia Minor in 451, but the same council also dealt a blow to his ambitions by declaring that the bishop of Constantinople had the same rights in the east as the bishop of Rome in the west. The political division was to be reflected in the organization of the church as well. But in 476 the western empire came to an end, and the Roman Senate recognized the eastern emperor once again.

The Roman Papacy Survives Many Challenges

The reconquest of Italy for the eastern empire under Justinian in the sixth century altered the pope's standing once more. Italy was ruled by the imperial representative, or exarch, from Ravenna, and Justinian himself interfered brutally and directly in the church's affairs. Rome was reduced to a minor bishopric on the edge of the eastern empire; the popes were usually Greek or Syrian. The city was even isolated from Ravenna by the Lombards, who conquered much of northern and central Italy. As a result of this isolation, the pope became the temporal as well as the religious ruler of Rome, and under Gregory I at the end of the sixth century the papacy's lands were reorganized on the lines of a great prince's estate. Gregory also acted as ruler of Rome in the emperor's name, paying armies and making peace treaties with the Lombards. Furthermore, his temporal successes enabled him to lay down the pattern for a church hierarchy which was controlled from the centre, with a clear chain of authority: bishops were to be answerable to archbishops, and archbishops answerable to the pope.

For the next century and a half the uneasy relationship between pope and eastern emperor persisted; when the empire was weak, the papacy gained in independence, at the expense of Rome being exposed to attack. But such attacks grew less likely as the tide of Arianism retreated. By the end of the seventh century the rulers, if not the common people, had returned to Catholicism, and the Lombards in Italy had been converted. The empire, on the other hand, had to face the rise of Moslem power, and had lost Syria and Egypt. At this point the most violent of the many theological controversies of these centuries erupted, when Leo the Isaurian, first of a new dynasty of emperors, banned the worship of images in 726. Popes Gregory II and III both resisted the iconoclasts, or image-breakers, as they were called; and in 733 Leo removed the dioceses of southern Italy and what is now Yugoslavia from the jurisdiction of Rome and transferred them to the see of Constantinople. This was coupled with the confiscation of the pope's estates there, and Rome's spiritual power seemed to be on the verge of collapse.

The Pope Decides to Seek Help from the Frankish King

But the imperial power in the west was also weak in the extreme, and renewed Lombard attacks led to the fall of Ravenna. Rome itself was threatened in 751 and it seemed that the papacy would soon fall under new Lombard masters, who were likely to be as harsh as the emperor. In this extremity, pope Stephen II, a Roman by birth, appealed to Pepin, the ruler of the Frankish kingdom. At a momentous meeting at Pepin's villa at Ponthion on 6 January 754, Pepin agreed to intervene. Furthermore, he agreed to 'restore' to the pope extensive lands in Italy which would make the papacy an independent principality. The whole political pattern of the medieval papacy stems from this agreement. The popes became bound to the Frankish royal house, who became their protectors, and they also became lords in central Italy, with secular interests and ambitions there. In theory, none of this need have affected their spiritual standing; in practice, it undoubtedly did. Pepin had reason to favour the church, since he owed his royal title to Stephen's predecessor Zacharias. Pepin, ruler in all but name, had deposed the last of the hereditary Merovingian dynasty, Childeric III. Faced by the problem of legalizing his position he had appealed to the pope, who, drawing on the example of Samuel and David in the Old Testament, had arranged for St Boniface to anoint him as king. Now Pepin repaid the debt by leading his army into Italy in 754 and again in 756. The Lombards were defeated, but the pope did not get the lands he had hoped for. Pepin's son Charles, known to us as Charlemagne, went further and overthrew the Lombard kings, becoming king of the Lombards himself. We shall look at Charlemagne's conquests later; as far as the popes were concerned, they found that they had in him a new Justinian; God had made him 'ruler of the Christian people', and on him depended 'the whole salvation of Christ's Church'. Like Constantine and Justinian before him, he interfered imperiously in church matters; when the iconoclastic dispute was settled in 787 with the approval of pope Hadrian I, Charlemagne summoned a council at Frankfurt to reverse the decision. When, in 795, Hadrian died, a new pope was chosen who was less likely to confront the king. On Christmas Day 800, Charlemagne was crowned emperor by the pope in St Peter's, apparently against his will, though Leo probably intended the gesture as a compliment. For the previous year Leo had been accused of perjury and adultery, and the question of who should judge the pope was brought up. In the event Charlemagne had accepted that no one could judge the pope, and he was allowed to clear himself by swearing an oath. But whatever Leo's motives in crowning Charlemagne, the latter saw that, if he accepted without protest, it would mean that the pope could dispose of the empire as he wished. Hence, when Charlemagne wished to ensure the succession of his son Louis, he crowned Louis himself at Aachen in 813. With hindsight, we can see that the stage was set for one of the central conflicts of medieval Europe: that between the papacy and the empire. The popes, in their most extreme moments, claimed that the emperors were subordinate to them, had their office from them, and could be deposed by them; the emperors retorted that the popes had no secular authority and could only intervene in spiritual affairs.

As Charlemagne's empire dissolved, so the papacy regained its independence. Nicholas I, in the mid ninth century, formulated the ideas about the relationship of papacy and empire which Leo's action had implied, and his successors claimed the right to depose unjust monarchs and to watch over the political actions of the emperors. But these high claims contrasted with a worsening of the situation in Italy; by the end of the ninth century, the popes had become playthings of the local politicians, ruling for a year or two, or no more than a matter of months, before they died, or, in several cases, were murdered. Many were nobles from the ruling families of Rome, and in the early eleventh century the counts of Tusculum nearly succeeded in turning the papacy into a hereditary office; brother succeeded brother; nephew succeeded uncle. It was only when the descendants of Charlemagne, the German sovereigns who ruled over his eastern lands and called themselves Holy Roman emperors, were powerful enough to intervene that the urgently needed reform of the papacy became possible. It was not until 1049, with the appointment by Henry III of Leo IX, a German bishop of noble birth, that the pope was once again a man of moral stature, concerned with spiritual and international affairs rather than mere local feuds.

Local Clergy Maintained Church Authority

John A.F. Thomson

While the pope was the head of the Roman Catholic Church, distance and the limits of communication it caused made it difficult for him to exert authority on a day-to-day basis. Instead, as church historian John A.F. Thomson points out in the following selection, bishops and other Christian leaders, or clerics, were the main representatives of the Church for most people. They were the ones who selected priests, encouraged the practice of proper rituals, and in general exercised jurisdiction over their dioceses, or church districts. Their practices varied according to local traditions.

Like the popes, however, bishops were not free from political influence. Political or lay leaders tried to keep the power to select bishops and other high-level clerics. They knew that such leaders held a great deal of status in their communities. Often, however, religious and lay leaders realized their common interests and were able to work together. Sometimes, in fact, as in the case of the Frankish King Louis the Pious, lay leaders seemed more devout than religious ones.

John A.F. Thomson is professor of medieval history at the University of Glasgow in Scotland.

One of the functions of the pope was that of bishop of Rome. As such he had a certain pre-eminence, but in the Church as a whole, other bishops could exercise similar functions in their own dioceses. Although effectively independent of any central authority, they might meet for consultations in local councils, normally summoned by the lay ruler, and pronounce collectively on matters of Church policy. In Dark Age Europe, and particularly after the barbarian invasions, when unified authority in the West had broken down, the local bishop represented continuity and order to his community, which was primarily an urban one—bishops were associated essentially with cities. The diocese was the basic unit of church organisation—it was to be a long time before a parish structure was developed at the more local level—and he himself was the crucial person in transmitting the faith. It was he who had the power to ordain priests and thereby secure the administration of the sacraments. This power of order was basic, but he normally acquired also a power of jurisdiction over his flock. In those parts of Western Europe where Christianity persisted from Roman times without a break, as in Frankish Gaul, local traditions were strong, and influential families which could trace their descent back to imperial times might well gain control over the office of bishop—many of the kindred of the chronicler Gregory of Tours were also bishops there, and their prominence in the Gaulish church went back before the barbarian conquests. It is clear, however, that the barbarian rulers came to terms with them, recognising that they had a useful part to play as influential local figures, not merely because of their spiritual role but also possibly because they could reconcile the existing Romanised population to their new masters. The large number of small Italian dioceses throughout the Middle Ages reflected the circumstances in which they were established in Roman times.

Christian Leadership in the Countryside

Not all areas which were Christianised, however, possessed towns, notably those regions beyond the imperial frontiers to which Christianity penetrated in the late Roman and sub-Roman periods. In Ireland, early dioceses can probably be equated with local petty kingdoms, but local churches were founded unsystematically, and the extent of episcopal authority, particularly compared with that of the abbot of the local great *monasterium* [monastery], has been a matter of considerable debate. This term, however, is an ambiguous one—it is significant that the two words 'monastery' and 'minster', which have distinct connotations, both derive from it—and certainly in some areas of Christendom, including Anglo-Saxon England, the occupants of such establishments were not always monks, who had withdrawn from the world, but priests who exercised a measure of local pastoral care, which was in the High Middle Ages taken over by the smaller parish unit. The laity were served by visiting clergy from these communities, who visited the surrounding countryside and preached to the people, possibly at places identified by standing crosses. Bede suggested that they might conduct baptisms, which was recognised as a priestly duty at the Council of Clofesho in 747. Indeed, it seems likely that the same establishments may in some cases have included both men whose devotion took the form of pious contemplation and others who undertook a more pastoral role, the two contrasted forms of religious observance which were to recur throughout the later history of the Church. In Anglo-Saxon England the bulk of clerics resided in larger centres of population, from which they extended their activity to surrounding rural areas.

It is important in any study of the Church at this period not to interpret words such as *monasterium* and *parochia* [parish] in their later sense, because this could be misleading. In the early period, the term *parochia* itself referred to an area much wider than that which it came to denote from the High Middle Ages onwards, and which possibly corresponded to secular administrative areas. In Scotland, indeed, the term *parochia* was still being equated with the territorial limits of the diocese of Glasgow as late as the mid-twelfth century, even though smaller local churches were being founded at this period. At an even later date it was employed to denote a mother church for an area with special baptismal rights. Increasingly parish limits were more stabilised from this date, and may well have been prompted by the parallel development of the new structures of feudal tenure in lay society, although there were later adjustments (both unions and divisions), usually in response to changes in the distribution of population. Significantly, however, there was administrative resistance to change because of the vested interests of existing parishes. Throughout Europe, however, there was no uniform pattern, and one suspects that in the early period, in the context of a missionary Church, practices varied according to immediate needs, and that it was only as it became more securely established that clearer administrative structures were set up. As this occurred the more centralised churches may have secured rights as centres of baptism and burial, which were only later devolved back to the local parish churches.

Before Christianity was given official recognition in the late Roman period, local communities had chosen their own leaders, and this practice continued to a later date, although, as discussed below, kings and aristocrats came to play an increasingly influential part in the choice of bishops. There were, however, disagreements over the nature of the office. Was a bishop to be seen as a prominent leader, who should appear as a man of dignity, or was an austere and humble saint to be preferred? Sulpicius Severus approved the humility of St Martin, and was embarrassed by another bishop who sat on his throne like an emperor's tribunal, but he reported that some men had opposed his consecration because his person was contemptible, his hair unkempt and his dress shabby. In Anglo-Saxon Northumbria, Bede praised the humility of St Aidan as bishop of Lindisfarne. But in an age in which the possession and display of the symbols of power was a means by which an individual's importance could be measured, bishops had to be seen as powerful figures. The Gaulish episcopate acquired many rights and privileges during the years of the invasions, and it was their ceremony which Wilfrid emulated when, at his consecration, he was borne into the oratory on a throne by nine bishops. With the passage of time, however, such pomp came to be regarded as unseemly. In the ninth century, Louis the Pious commanded bishops and clerics to give up girdles adorned with golden belts and jewelled daggers, regarding it as monstrous that a representative of the Church should aspire to the accoutrements of worldly glory.

Who Has the Right to Choose Bishops—the Church or Local Political Leaders?

The bishops' prominence in their communities was liable to draw them into secular affairs, so it is hardly surprising that lay rulers were concerned at their choice. Gregory of Tours tells that in the early sixth century St Nicetius was consecrated as bishop of Trier with the consent of the people and by the decree of the king. In the middle of the century a dispute over the succession to the see of Clermont demonstrates even more clearly where real power lay. A locally elected candidate tried to assume full powers before he was fully inducted into office, but a council of bishops, meeting under royal auspices, chose an alternative, who was favourably received by the people. It was the latter who secured the post. Two points about this episode are worth noting; the local community's views were still considered, even when their original preference had been set aside, but the king was able to influence them, and was able to rely on a council of bishops to assist him. Indeed, the bishops' importance in the social and political structure of Merovingian Gaul is reflected in the way in which the chronicler Fredegar groups them, almost automatically, with the lay magnates as the kings' principal advisers.

Such lay influence reflected the reality of power in the West, which diverged from the theoretical assertion of ecclesiastical independence in the general councils of the Church. The second Council of Nicaea (787) laid down that the election of a bishop, priest or deacon brought about by a lay ruler should be void, and the fourth Council of Constantinople (869–70) condemned the nomination of bishops through the intrigues of the civil power. The accepted procedure envisaged at the earlier of these councils was that they should be chosen by their fellow bishops in a province, with the proceedings being confirmed by a metropolitan. These provisions probably reflect a more developed hierarchy in the East than was found in the contemporary Western Church, although some aspects of this approach may also have applied in the West. The Clermont case, cited earlier, suggests a procedure for consulting existing bishops, even at a time when popular assent was still regarded as necessary. One cannot assume uniformity of practice throughout the whole Church, and it is perhaps necessary to distinguish between those lands with a continuous tradition of Christianity and those which had been recently converted. In England and Germany, the Papacy played an important part in appointing bishops in the period of the early missions, but as the Church became firmly established the interest of the lay power in appointing bishops increased. In England as early as 666 Wine was alleged to have bought the see of London from the king of Mercia, but in the following year the pope nominated Theodore of Tarsus as archbishop of Canterbury, perhaps taking advantage of the fact that an archbishop elect, sent for ordination by the kings of Kent and Northumbria, had died in Rome. Royal influence was very clear in the choice of the first archbishop of York, Egbert, who was of royal blood and whose brother Eadberht succeeded to the Northumbrian throne in 738. Although Alcuin states that Egbert's successor was elected by popular acclaim, it would be surprising if he had been chosen without royal approval. Royal influence was clearly demonstrated in the mid-eighth century, when King Offa of Mercia had the principal see of his immediate kingdom, that of Lichfield, raised to the status of an archbishopric, a position which it failed to retain when Mercia went into decline. In Spain, where King Reccared had played a decisive part in turning his kingdom from Arianism to Catholic Christianity, he and his successors summoned a series of church councils, or in some cases attracted criticism for failing to do so. King Sisebut imposed a bishop on the see of Barcelona, and rebuked a bishop of Tarragona for being too interested in the theatre, while by the end of the seventh century Erwig established a system by which the king chose and the metropolitan of Toledo approved candidates for episcopal vacancies.

In the last resort, the Church needed the protection of the lay rulers, and in return it had to concede substantial influence to them. A well-disposed king could strengthen it, for lay influence was not always as malign as the church reformers of the eleventh century were to suggest, indeed asserting their views so successfully that these have coloured retrospectively much historical thought on the earlier period. Einhard paid tribute to the piety of Charlemagne, and Asser did the same for Alfred of Wessex. The fact that kings were consecrated gave them a quasi-clerical status, which strengthened their moral authority in dealing with Church affairs.

Organizing the Monasteries

Roger Collins

In addition to the papacy, various monastic orders
worked to spread Christianity during the Early Middle
Ages. Monasteries, in fact, became an important part of
the Church's institutional structure. They became centers
of education and scholarship as well as religion. Moreover, monks served as missionaries to western Europe's
remaining pagans.

Among the more famous leaders of the monastic movement was Benedict who lived from 480 to 544. His work
was acknowledged by Pope Gregory I, who was later
known as Gregory the Great and who had himself been a
monk. Gregory, pope from 590 to 604, claimed that Benedict's *Rule*, a document that sought to regulate monks'
lives, should be a guide for all Christians.

In the following selection, however, Roger Collins
notes that the monastic movement was much broader
than Benedict's list of regulations might allow. Monasticism was adopted from the Near East, where isolation
and meditation had long been important for the deeply
religious. Western Christian leaders such as St. Augustine
altered the practice. In the west, monasticism became oriented around groups of monks rather than individuals. In
addition, monastic groups were often formed by the
wealthy and powerful, who sought to demonstrate their
devotion to Christianity. All in all, Collins suggests,
monasticism was far more varied than Benedict seemed
to recognize.

Roger Collins, a former university instructor, is the author of four books on medieval history.

Excerpted from Roger Collins, *Early Medieval Europe: 300–1000*. Copyright © 1991
Roger Collins. Reprinted with permission from Macmillan Publishers Ltd.

When Augustine became bishop of Hippo in 395 he established a house-monastery in which to live with his immediate episcopal entourage and from which he would carry out the various pastoral and administrative duties of his new office. He may have been one of the first western bishops to do this, but he was adopting a tradition already well established in the East. Noted bishops and theologians such as the three 'Cappadocian Fathers'—Basil, bishop of Caesarea, his brother Gregory of Nyssa, and their friend Gregory of Nazianzus—had set up 'private' monastic institutions on their own property and had attempted to combine office in the Church with continuing personal commitment to an ascetic life. Under their inspiration a number of laymen created similar monastic households.

From the late fourth century this was also the way in which many monastic institutions developed in the West. Wealthy individuals or families decided, under the inspiration of the ideal of achieving personal salvation through renunciation and the leading of a disciplined and regulated life of prayer, meditation, and good works, to turn their houses into monasteries in which they would live with selected companions, following a pattern of such a life of their own devising. The founders of such establishments were almost always wealthy, in that they depended on their own financial resources to create them, though it is possible in some cases that communities were set up on deserted or unclaimed land.

A number of bishops, especially in Gaul, founded and endowed monastic houses, over which they themselves did not preside. Instead they appointed abbots to govern them. Such institutions were intended to be permanent, in a way that aristocratic household monasteries might not be. It would be unwise, however, to draw too many distinctions between such establishments. In some cases founders of 'private' monastic houses were subsequently persuaded into accepting episcopal office, and then turned their private foundations into regular and permanent monasteries. For example, Martin, bishop of Tours founded Ligugé, south of Poitiers, prior to his episcopal election, and then after his ordination set up another monastery at Marmoutier on the

Loire from which to direct his diocese.

A similar case is that of the famous island monastery of Lérins, near Cannes on the Côte d'Azure. This was founded by Honoratus, a member of a Gallic aristocratic family. He attracted a growing number of followers willing to join him, and when he was persuaded to become bishop

---

A Monk's Primary Duty Is Obedience

Benedict's Rule was very clear in directing that monks obey not only the word of God but also the word of their superiors.

The first degree of humility is prompt obedience. This is required of all who, whether by reason of the holy servitude to which they are pledged, or through fear of hell, or to attain to the glory of eternal life, hold nothing more dear than Christ. Such disciples delay not in doing what is ordered by their superior, just as if the command had come from God. Of such our Lord says, *At the hearing of the ear he hath obeyed me.* And to the teachers He likewise says, *He that heareth you, heareth me.*

For this reason such disciples, surrendering forthwith all they possess, and giving up their own will, leave unfinished what they were working at, and with the ready foot of obedience in their acts follow the word of command. Thus, as it were, at the same moment comes the order of the master and the finished work of the disciple: with the speed of the fear of God both go jointly forward and are quickly effected by such as ardently desire to walk in the way of eternal life. These take the narrow way, of which the Lord saith, *Narrow is the way which leads to life.* That is, they live not as they themselves will, neither do they obey their own desires and pleasures; but following the command and direction of another and abiding in their monasteries, their desire is to be ruled by an abbot. Without doubt such as these carry out that saying of our Lord, *I came not to do my own will, but the will of Him Who sent me.*

Selection from Benedict, *Rule*, reprinted in *The Early Middle Ages: 500–1000*, ed. Robert Brentano. New York: Macmillan/Free Press, 1964.

of Arles in 427 he appointed one of them, Maximus, to succeed him as head of the community. In turn Maximus became bishop of Riez in 433, and his successor as abbot of Lérins, Faustus, in due course also took over his episcopal see. By this time Lérins had established itself as probably the most influential monastic house in the Rhône basin and Provence. Others of its products, and not necessarily former abbots, were sought for episcopal appointments throughout the region. One of these, Caesarius, bishop of Arles founded a major monastic house for women in his diocesan city, and wrote a rule for its inmates.

Such monasteries were frequently urban, but a number also came to be set up on rural family estates. Cassiodorus retired to his country property at Vivarium in the south of Italy after the final elimination of the Ostrogothic kingdom, and set up such a monastery there. For the monks he admitted to it to live under his direction he wrote his *Institutes*, providing advice on what they should read and how they should copy books and check their doctrinal orthodoxy and textual accuracy. Many such monasteries cannot have survived the death of their founders, but from the sixth century onwards it became increasingly common for those who set up such houses to try to ensure their continuance by committing the regulations under which their inmates lived to writing, to guarantee that the rule of life by which they lived would be preserved. In some cases these may have been no more than the Latin translations of some of the Greek monastic rules produced by Basil of Caesarea and others.

Creating Rules for Monks and Monasteries

Fuller and more comprehensive sets of regulations did, however, start to appear in the West by the sixth century. Amongst the earliest of these is the anonymous work known as *The Rule of the Master*, written around the year 525, possibly somewhere in the vicinity of Rome. Slightly later in date and in part dependent on *The Rule of the Master* is the more famous *Rule of Benedict*. This work is the first of the major western rules whose author is known, at least in so far as the testimony of some of the manuscripts of the work may be believed. Biographical information concerning this Benedict derives from the account of him in Book II of pope Gregory the Great's *Dialogues*, a series of stories concerning the lives and miracles of recent Italian holy men, written in 593.

It would be unwise to place much reliance on the details of Gregory's stories concerning Benedict, which were intended to be didactic and edifying. Only the barest outline of his life can in fact be drawn. Benedict (*c.* 480–547) is said to have been educated in Rome but to have retired into a spiritual retreat in a cave at Subiaco around the age of twenty. He is reported to have founded some twelve monastic communities in the area over the next few years and to have received the children of a number of senators from Rome for education. He subsequently moved further south and established his most famous monastic community on the site of a former pagan temple on Monte Cassino in the Apennines north-west of Capua around the year 529.

The *Rule* composed by Benedict for the observance of his monks has aroused much—and sometimes excessive—adulation. It is important to appreciate that in the sixth and seventh centuries it was one amongst a number of such rules, composed in Italy, Gaul, Spain and Ireland, and that its general dissemination throughout western Europe as the principal blueprint for the monastic life was largely the result of Carolingian attempts in the early ninth century to establish uniform patterns of monastic, canonical and liturgical observance. Although less ferocious in its discipline than the majority of early medieval Irish monastic rules, the twelve 'degrees of humility' propounded by *The Rule of Benedict* add up to the image of a society that is absolutist and totalitarian.

No modern dictator could hope to control the minds and behaviour of his subjects in quite the way that Benedict's abbot should be able to. The individual monk was required to be obedient to his abbot in all things, to have no will of his own, not to complain about any injuries or ill-treatment to which he might be subjected when under obedience, to 'be content with the meanest and worst of everything', to call himself and think of himself as being the lowest of the low, to take no independent action, not to speak except in reply to a superior and to avoid laughter.

Benedict's *Rule*, like that of 'the Master', was unusual in its own time for being so all-embracing in terms of the aspects of the monastic life it sought to regulate. The anonymous or pseudonymous rules that were followed in the monasteries of southern Gaul tended to remain closer to eastern originals, in that they were concerned more with the nature of the spiritual instruction to be provided and less with the minutiae of the practicalities of communal life. That the *Rule of Benedict* would emerge as the best known and most widely used of all western monastic rules was probably less a product of its intrinsic merits than the chance combination of the way it came to the attention of one of the most significant and influential of early medieval popes, and its subsequent influence, albeit mixed with indigenous traditions, on the Irish Church. Both of these were also to play a significant role in the development of the missionary ventures of the seventh and eighth centuries.

A Monk Becomes Pope Gregory I

Of the popes of the early middle ages Gregory I (590–604)— known as 'the Great'—is by far the most outstanding. In part this may be a reflection of the fact that more is known about him than about virtually all of his predecessors and most of his successors before the twelfth century. The survival of approximately 850 of his official letters provides an extraordinary amount of insight into both the practical problems he faced during his pontificate and the working of his mind. To this can be added the substantial corpus of his exegetical writings, composed during his period as papal representative in Constantinople and in the opening years of his period as pope.

Most, if indeed not all, of these were composed for monastic audiences and readers. For where Gregory was truly novel was in being the first pope who had previously been a monk. He belonged in this respect to the tradition of the founders of aristocratic 'house-monasteries', having turned his family house on the Caelian Hill into a monastery. Like a number of bishops, he also maintained a modified monastic lifestyle during his pontificate. It was from his monastery on the Caelian that he drew the group of monks whom he sent under Augustine to evangelise the Anglo-Saxon kingdom of Kent in 596.

The subsequent history of missionary ventures has often been seen as a symbiosis between Irish monasticism and the Roman traditions deriving from Gregory's venture in sending monks to Kent. The apparent propensity of the Anglo-Saxon Church from the later seventh century onwards for producing missionaries anxious to spread the Gospel to the pagans east of the Rhine (not least their own continental Saxon 'relatives') is seen in this perspective as a consequence of these twin elements in its own genesis. In turn the special ties that linked the Anglo-Saxons to the Papacy became the route through which the Frankish rulers, under whose political aegis the missionaries had to work, renewed their contacts with Rome. From these derived not least the papal support for the replacement of the Merovingian dynasty by the Carolingian in 751 and ultimately the coronation of the second king of this line as the new Roman emperor in the year 800.

This pattern of relationships at least has the virtue of neatness. However, the reality of the past is rarely as tidy as historians' reconstructions of it, and this particular set of events is a case in point. Although both Irish monasticism and the Papacy had roles to play in the expansion of Latin Christianity and in the political and cultural realignments of eighth century Francia, it is dangerous to highlight these to such an extent that other elements are obscured or concealed.

Chapter 2

The German and Hun Invasions

Turning|Points

IN WORLD HISTORY

The Germanic Tribes and the Roman Empire

David Nicholas

As the Roman Empire expanded into northern Europe, Romans encountered the various Germanic peoples who inhabited these regions. As time passed, the Romans tried to bring elements of their civilization to the Germanic tribes, as well as incorporate them into their army and administration.

In the following selection, historian David Nicholas asserts that, when compared to the highly civilized Romans, the Germanic peoples lived at a seminomadic, tribal level. The Germanic tribes' migrations, which sometimes brought them into conflict with the empire as well as with each other, were conducted mainly to find new hunting or grazing grounds. Moreover, as Nicholas points out, Germanic peoples had a limited conception of effective political leadership as well as law. Instead, their societies were organized around war and kinship. Finally, even after the Germans were converted to Christianity, they combined Christian ritual with earlier tribal "superstitions."

David Nicholas, an expert on medieval Europe, is professor of history at Clemson University.

The first traces of the Germanic tribes which were eventually to succeed the Roman Empire are found in Scandinavia around 1000 B.C. The migration was gradual and spasmodic, and only in the last centuries B.C. did the Germans replace the Celts as the dominant ethnic group of northern Europe. They were occupying lands adjacent to the Roman Empire when Julius Caesar began his conquest of Gaul in 58 B.C.

Excerpted from David Nicholas, *The Medieval West, 400–1450: A Preindustrial Civilization.* Copyright © 1973 The Dorsey Press. Reprinted with permission from the author.

During the centuries after the Roman occupation, Mediterranean influences began to penetrate and "civilize" the Germanic world. Trade was initiated by Roman merchants along the Rhine-Danube line. The Germans began to acquire a veneer of Roman culture and imitated Roman behavior, just as "chic" Romans of the late Empire were to play decadence games by imitating German dress and customs. During the years of quiet on the line, while movement southwest seemed permanently halted, migrations continued within the Germanic world as tribes sought better land or hunting.

The invasions were not monolithic. Numerous tribes appear in Caesar's *Gallic Wars* which were not among those entering the empire in the third century A.D. and after. Confederations were apparently formed and new names assumed easily. There never was a deliberate attempt to overthrow the Roman empire as a political entity. The Germanic wanderings into Gaul in the late Empire were simply the last stage in the gradual migration in search of better conditions which had begun toward 1000 B.C.

The Germans began moving again as early as the 160s, when the Marcomanni and Quadi invaded northern Italy. They were pushed back, but with some effort. The Germans broke the lines again for two decades during the disastrous third century, a period which saw considerable change in the Germanic world. New tribal groupings were formed which were to last into the fifth century.

Small Groups of Rural Tribespeople

The Germanic tribes were always small. Anthropologists have compared the Franks at the time of Clovis (481–511) to the American Indians at the time of Columbus. Their forms of livelihood were so primitive that a high population density could not be sustained. Except in northern Gaul and what is now Germany west of the Rhine, the Germans were always a minority among the populations with whom they settled, a fact which explains the impermanence of many tribal kingdoms.

There was tremendous variation in economic activity, social structure, language, and religion among the tribes. Caesar and the Roman historian Tacitus, who wrote his *Germania* at the end of the first century A.D., have titillated historians' imaginations by their picturesque descriptions of blond beasts living in a primitive democratic society with all rugged virtues. This is romanticism, but the historian can learn much from these writers.

Caesar described migratory tribesmen who were basically herdsmen. Whether the Germans were practicing settled agriculture in the first century B.C. is uncertain, but they definitely were by Tacitus' time. They knew a sort of communal agrarian regime in forest clearings with common use of implements, but they also recognized private property and class distinctions. Although they were familiar with Roman coins, they used them chiefly for decoration and as a sort of wampum, not for exchange as money. Roman merchants handled all trade of the Germans with the outside world. The Germans had basically a subsistence economy based on the land, and this was to continue even after the migrations had ended. While the Germans were later to use Roman towns as fortresses, and some kings may have used them as winter quarters, Germans rarely inhabited towns as traders before the mid-seventh century. They did have some industry, but it was very utilitarian until the seventh century and consisted chiefly of pottery and weapons. Only in the seventh century did the Germans of northern Europe begin to develop artistic skills which they applied to their own tastes—more abstract and linear than the Roman—and even then much of their artisanry simply dealt with finely ornamented weapons and jewelry. The primitive German loved the bright and shiny and had little sense of economic value.

The Germans were very superstitious when they entered the empire, and there is no evidence that they became less so after they adopted Christianity. Their gods were deities of the forest. Trees were sacred to many tribes. Frankish burial customs even from the Christian period show much of the pagan background. The warrior was often buried in full battle costume, with his weapons and provisions for his future life. Even among the most orthodox and best educated there was an almost universal belief in demons, magic, and witchcraft.

Primitive Kingship and Law

Most Germanic tribes had kings by the fifth century, usually chosen by the great men of the tribe. Some monarchs managed to make the position hereditary in their families, but elective kingship persisted and was a fundamental weakness of early medieval monarchy, and of the German monarchy throughout the Middle Ages. The presence of a king in no way implies a well-developed concept of the state. Certainly if the primitive Germans lacked an idea of the state, they had borrowed one from the Romans by the time their law codes were compiled in the late fifth, sixth, and seventh centuries, but the concept was very rudimentary. Although these codes recognize the kindred's right of vengeance and the fundamental duty of the culprit to pay compensation to the injured man according to his status and degree of damage, they did reserve a certain percentage of most fines to the king, a fact which implies some administrative organization. Different ethnic groups had their own law. The Visigothic king Alaric II compiled a *Breviary* of Roman law for his subjects in southwestern France which was to be the major source of Roman legal practice known in the west before the late 11th century. The Burgundians had two separate laws, for themselves and for their Roman subjects. Although the Germans tried to operate what was left of the Roman administrative and judicial system, and particularly the tax structure, they hopelessly lacked the means, and government declined into an essentially local concern. Kingship and kingdom were regarded less as a state than as the personal possession of the monarch, at whose death the normal rules of inheritance would apply, with the sons dividing the spoils equally.

The Germanic judicial system was a blend of the picturesque and the picaresque. Local juries were used as fact-swearing boards, but God was the judge. The *mallus*, the local assembly of the free men of the tribe, was extremely important in some tribes, and in most it had a judicial function. Charlemagne established a permanent body of men who knew the law, the *scabini*, from among the free men of each locality, but by this time there were fewer free men than before, and tribes had become so fragmented that the *mallus* was of little effect in government. There was no distinction between jury and worldly judge, for the *scabini* were both. There was no concept of trial before impartial persons who knew nothing of the deeds; these juries knew either the law or the facts of the situation, and preferably both. If a defendant admitted his guilt in a criminal case, he paid the prescribed fine or underwent mutilation. If he maintained his innocence, he submitted to trial by ordeal. There were several forms of this. A priest might bless a piece of hot iron which the defendant would then carry for a certain distance. His burns would be certified and bound by the priest. If his wound seemed to be healing after a few days, he was judged innocent. Similarly, the priest might bless a stream into which the defendant was thrown; if he sank, the waters received him and he was considered innocent, but a guilty man floated. Some persons, chiefly men of high social status such as priests and aristocrats, might clear themselves by personal oath of innocence or by the use of oath-helpers. A certain number of persons would be required to swear to the innocence of the accused, with the number varying according to the social status of the oath-helpers and the defendant, and the nature of the crime. Obviously those with extended kindreds and/or personal retinues could get oath-helpers easily, while lesser men had more trouble. Although other forms of proof gradually were introduced as rulers began to suspect that God might need the help of trustworthy witnesses, the ordeal ended only when the Fourth Lateran Council forbade the clergy to participate in such proceedings in 1215. Since supernatural sanction was the basis of the whole system, the ordeal went out of use as a trial procedure.

Among the Germans, Family Relationships Meant Most

Although the Germans had an embryonic idea of the state, their society was fundamentally based upon a system of private contract at all levels. Chief among these arrangements was the kindred. In an age of total breakdown, everyone needed protection, and the kindred could provide at least the safety of numbers. "Kindred" meant "extended family" and was a much more inclusive term than it is today. When an individual was injured or killed, his kindred had the right and duty to obtain compensation from the malefactors according to tribal custom. They might choose instead to declare the blood feud and hunt down the culprit and his entire kindred to the death. Much of the effort of Germanic kings to keep order in their realms, insofar as they bothered about such things at all, dealt not with the limitation or abolition of the dominant role of the kindred, which remained a strong bond in criminal justice in German Europe throughout the Middle Ages, but rather with an attempt to force the injured party and/or his kindred to accept customary compensation if offered by the other side. The Germanic law codes show us not a bucolic paradise of primitive democracy, but a jungle in which there was a price on every man's head, varying with his social status. This meant essentially that a powerful man might murder whomever he pleased if he paid the man's *wergeld* (worth money), but the less powerful would think twice about the effects on their resources of the murder of a powerful man with a powerful kindred. Except among the most mighty, the kindred was only partially successful in giving protection. Hence, particularly as the tribes settled down, the band of retainers, bound by loyalty to a lord rather than by the blood tie, began to take the place of the kindred, but never did so totally. Loyalty to someone more powerful than oneself and one's kindred could provide the two essentials of the medieval existence—protection and livelihood.

Hence the war band surrounding the great men of the tribes was a fundamental social unit. The warriors were sworn to follow the lord to the death. The highest social status was reserved for the warrior who distinguished himself by service to a greater man than himself, one who could bestow lands, offices, and social distinction. A sort of prestige hierarchy developed among war bands, with the royal *comitatus* (following) at the top. But these groups fluctuated. Faithful service was rewarded by the major source of wealth

of the lord—land—and when a warrior received lands he became less mobile and willing to follow his lord about at all
times. Accordingly, the place of some warriors was taken by
persons who could still gain by association with the king,
while the older group of warriors could gain more by opposition to the king than by service to him. Service to a greater
man hence did not in itself make a man without other distinction into an aristocrat, but it was a means of amassing
property and dependents of his own, the signs of a life style
of a great person.

Below the war bands in prestige were persons who
worked the land. The free peasant was also a warrior during
the campaigning season; but since the campaigning season
and the growing season were the same, military service was
a burden. This group accordingly tended to sink into serfdom, giving up their freedom to persons who would protect
them and do military service on their behalf. Particularly in
England and Germany, however, some free peasants persisted. . . . The tone of Germanic society was given by warfare, within and between tribes, and the warriors hence
dominated. Germanic society was highly stratified, with numerous technical gradations given in the law codes even
within the general groups of free and unfree, but despite this
fact it was easier to move from one class to another on the
basis of strength, intelligence, or increased wealth than it became later. The blood tie was all-important with the Germans, as with all primitive peoples, but it did not necessarily
affect the social status of descendants.

The Germans and Huns Could Destroy but Not Lead

Joseph R. Strayer

In the fourth and fifth centuries, Europe was beset by a series of invasions from central Asian nomadic peoples
known as Huns. Not only did these invasions disturb the
boundaries of the Roman Empire, they inspired new migrations among the various Germanic tribes, who were
seeking to avoid the Huns.

The Romans tried to incorporate these German groups
into their army, and in 451 a combined German and
Roman force fought off an invasion by Attilla the Hun.
However, as Joseph R. Strayer points out in the following
selection from his history of medieval Europe, the alliance
was very uneasy. One group of Germans, the Visigoths,
turned against the Romans, sacking Rome itself in 410.
Other Germanic tribes such as the Vandals, Ostrogoths,
Franks, Angles, and Saxons began to carve new kingdoms
out of Roman territories.

Strayer goes on to claim that while some mixing between Germanic and Roman peoples and traditions occurred, the Germans were not sophisticated enough to
reinvigorate western European culture. The final triumph
of the Germanic peoples, after the fall of the last western
Roman emperor in 476, marked the beginning of what
many have called the Dark Ages.

Joseph R. Strayer was professor of history at Princeton
University for many years.

Potential invaders could be found everywhere on the long
frontiers of the Empire, but in the fourth and fifth centuries

Excerpted from Joseph R. Strayer, *Western Europe in the Middle Ages: A Short History.* Copyright © 1955 Appleton-Century-Crofts, Inc.

Rome's most dangerous neighbors were the Germans of Central and Eastern Europe. They were familiar enough with conditions in the Empire to covet its material resources and to realize its political and military weakness. For centuries they had been filtering across the border into the promised land, raiding when Rome was weak, enlisting in the army when she was strong. Many Roman generals and most of their troops were German, and the nominally Roman provinces along the Rhine and Danube were full of semi-civilized German tribes which had been conquered and settled in strategic locations as frontier guards.

This natural drift of Germans into the Empire was greatly accelerated in the fourth century by the sudden irruption of the Huns into Eastern Europe. The Huns were one of those nomadic peoples of Central Asia whose periodic raids have repeatedly changed the history of the great coastal civilizations of the Eurasian landmass. Ordinarily scattered and disunited, the nomads were occasionally brought together by able leaders, and when this happened they formed an almost irresistible force. Tireless and tough, inured to extremes of heat and cold, content with meager rations, spending most of their waking hours in the saddle, hitting hard and suddenly, they could be defeated only by well-disciplined troops operating under first-rate commanders. The Germans, in spite of their bravery as individuals, could offer no effective resistance to the Huns, and the wedge of nomad invaders drove through the strongest Germanic peoples into the heart of Europe. Many of the Germans became subjects or tributaries of the Huns; those who escaped this fate milled around frantically looking for a place of safety. The most obvious refuge was behind the fortified lines of the Roman frontier, and tremendous pressure built up all along the border. From the Rhine delta to the Black Sea the Germans were on the move, and the Roman government could do nothing to stop them.

Rome Is Sacked by the Visigoths

Since the Germans could not be stopped, the obvious move was to regularize the situation by admitting them as allies serving in the Roman army. This policy was followed with the Visigoths, the first group to cross the frontier. It was not entirely successful, since the Visigoths became annoyed at being treated as a subject people and repeatedly revolted, asking for more land, more pay, and higher offices for their leaders. They defeated a Roman army at Adrianople in 378; they pillaged the western Balkans and moved into Italy, where they sacked Rome in 410. Then they were persuaded to continue their migration to Spain, where they drove out another group of invaders and set up a Visigothic kingdom. In spite of these excesses, the bond between the Visigoths and the Roman government was never entirely broken. They served the Empire occasionally in wars with other Germanic peoples and one of their kings died, fighting for Rome, in a great battle against the Huns in 451.

Meanwhile, the push across the frontiers continued. The Vandals marched from central Germany, through Gaul and Spain, to North Africa. The Burgundians occupied the valley of the Rhône. A mercenary army in Italy set up a king of their own in 476, the traditional date of the fall of the Empire in the West. The emperor at Constantinople could find no remedy for this situation except to send a new group of Germans, the Ostrogoths, against the usurper. The Ostrogoths, under their great leader Theodoric, were successful, but the Empire gained little, for Theodoric promptly created a kingdom for himself in Italy. Last of all, the Franks began to occupy Gaul, while the Angles and Saxons started the slow conquest of Britain.

The occupation of the Western provinces by the Germans caused less material damage than might have been expected. Almost everywhere the imperial government succeeded in keeping some sort of connection with the leaders of the occupying forces. German kings were made generals in the Roman army, given honorary titles such as consul or patrician, or even adopted into the imperial family. These were not mere face-saving devices, since they kept the Germans from treating their new possessions as conquered territory. The Romans in the West preserved their law, as much of their local government as they desired, and most of their property. The Germans had to be given land, but the West, with its thin population, had land to spare, and few of the old inhabitants had to be completely dispossessed. There was a considerable amount of pillaging and violence while the Germans were moving through the Empire, but once they had settled down they were not hostile to the Romans. There had never been any deep-rooted racial or cultural antagonism between Roman and German. Intermarriages had been and continued to be common, and the Germans had great respect for Roman civilization, as far as they understood it. They had come into the Empire to enjoy it, not to destroy it; they had not the slightest idea of wiping out the old way of life and substituting a new Germanic culture in its place.

A New Europe

And yet the coming of the Germans did mark the end of Roman civilization in the West. In some regions, especially along the Rhine and upper Danube, the Germans settled so thickly that the few remaining Romans could not preserve their language and customs. Britain, which had never been completely Romanized, lost practically all of its Latin civilization during the Anglo-Saxon conquest. The Romans had withdrawn their garrisons and officials before the Saxons arrived, so that there was no way to arrange for a peaceful transfer of authority. The native Britons reverted to their Celtic culture, but while this gave them enough courage to resist, it did not give them enough strength to defeat the invaders. They were forced back into the mountains, or driven to France, where they gave the name of Brittany to the Armorican peninsula. In Italy, Spain, and most of Gaul, the Germans were never numerous enough to change the fundamental characteristics of the population, but even in these regions there was a profound alteration in the organization of society and the activities of the people. Roman institutions and culture had been decaying for two centuries in the West, and the Germans were not able to put new life into a senile civilization. They were intelligent enough as individuals, but they lacked the traditions, the institutions, and the training which was necessary to understand and reinvigorate the relatively complicated system over which they had gained control. . . .

The Germans lacked the political experience and traditions necessary to build strong states on the ruins of the Roman Empire. They were equally unable to solve the economic problems of the ancient world. Even more than the Romans, they had sought local self-sufficiency; each German village had to supply itself with the essentials of life. They had imported a few luxuries from their neighbors, but there had never been active trade in common necessities. When they entered the Empire they could not alter the prevailing pattern of economic activity. They took over Roman estates and continued the Roman luxury trade with the East, but they certainly did not increase production or trade. Western Europe continued to be an almost purely agricultural region with few economic ties among its provinces.

The Terror of the German Barbarians

The Roman historian Ammianus Marcellus reported on the way Germanic warriors inspired fear among Roman soldiers. This passage is from his chronicle of the Roman defeat at the hands of the Visigoths at the battle of Adrianople in 378.

And so the barbarians, their eyes blazing with frenzy, were pursuing our men, in whose veins the blood was chilled with numb horror: some fell without knowing who struck them down, others were buried beneath the mere weight of their pursuers, and some were slain by the sword of a comrade; for though they often rallied, there was no ground given, nor did anyone spare those who retreated. Besides all this, the roads were blocked by many who lay mortally wounded, lamenting the torment of their wounds; and with them also mounds of fallen horses filled the plains with corpses. To these ever irreparable losses, so costly to the Roman state, a night without the bright light of the moon put an end.

Selection from *Ammianus Marcellus, The Eagle, the Crescent, and the Cross: Sources of Medieval History*, Volume I, ed. Charles T. Davis. New York: Appleton-Century-Crofts, 1967 edition.

A Cultural Decline

The same decline may be observed in intellectual and literary activities. The Roman tradition had lost most of its vitality, and the German tradition was not sufficiently developed to be used as a substitute. The Romans of the Late Empire were content with what had been done before. They imitated Virgil and Suetonius; they wrote commentaries on classical works of literature; they prepared encyclopedias which contained all essential knowledge in a few hundred pages. The Germans had their legendary stories and poems, but they could not believe that these barbaric productions were equal in value to the highly polished, sophisticated Roman works. The German stories survived as part of the oral tradition of the northern peoples, but it was centuries before most of them were written down. Meanwhile, there was great respect for the Roman intellectual and literary tradition, but little understanding of it. Few of the Germans ever mastered the art of reading Latin, and the great majority of the Romans cared as little for the survival of their literature as they did for the survival of the imperial government. The only learning that was absolutely essential was some knowledge of grammar and syntax and some knowledge of private law. These needs could be met by the preparation of little books of excerpts which illustrated rules of language or of jurisprudence. Even this limited intellectual activity was too much of an effort for most of the inhabitants of Western Europe, and by 800 an educated layman was rarely found outside of Italy.

The Germanic Tribes Split Rome Apart

Stephen Williams and Gerard Friell

Ever since the Romans had begun adding Germanic territories to their empire, they had sought to turn the Germans into supporters and allies. By the third and fourth centuries, as the empire suffered from internal problems ranging from bad leadership to ever-greater disparities of wealth, the Germans' roles in Rome were growing larger. This was particularly true for the army.

Indeed, as Stephen Williams and Gerard Friell point out in the following excerpt from their book on the Roman Emperor Theodosius, the Germanic tribes had become important sources of soldiers for Rome's army. Sometimes, Germanic officers even served as Roman officers. By the fifth century, it was difficult in the western empire to tell the Roman and Germanic armies apart. In addition, the Germanic tribes had grown more aggressive in the wake of the Hun invasions, seeking safer lands and beneficial alliances with the Romans and others.

Germanic aggressiveness helped to make Roman authority in the west weaker, and Germanic leaders pushed their advantages. By the mid-fifth century, Germans were demanding high-level positions in Rome's army and administration, as well as land and plunder. Needing allies themselves, Roman leaders often had no choice but to give in to German demands. Even when the final western emperor was deposed in 476, Germans already in fact controlled western Europe.

Stephen Williams and Gerard Friell are the authors of several articles on the Roman Empire as well as two books: *Theodosius: The Empire at Bay* and *The Rome That Did Not Fall*.

Excerpted from Stephen Williams and Gerard Friell, *Theodosius: The Empire at Bay*. Copyright © 1994 Stephen Williams and Gerard Friell. Reprinted with permission from Yale University Press.

The large historical questions do not go away, but they easily relapse into vacuity, question begging or, at least, lack of focus. There is little point in rummaging yet again among the fifty-seven causes of the Fall of the Western Roman Empire until we have well-defined questions and as explicit as possible a frame of reference.

The dismemberment of the West was not a cataclysmic event. The sack of Rome in A.D. 410, to take the most hackneyed example, was quite avoidable, and was—in any case—of psychological rather than strategic importance. Nonetheless, if we take an arbitrary period of roughly half a century between the death of Valentinian I in 375 and the occupation of Africa by the Vandals in 429–30, we cannot possibly deny that profound and seemingly irreversible changes have occurred.

At the beginning of this period imperial power and authority are dominant within the traditionally defined frontiers, and are regularly projected beyond them into barbarian territory through successful campaigns. Its rule is in many ways predatory and oppressive, but nobody within or outside the empire doubts its reality. There are many Germanic newcomers settled in the provinces, but they are subordinate to Roman administration. Many of the soldiers, officers and generals of the Roman army are themselves of Germanic origin, but their command structures, ambitions and loyalties are firmly Roman. Pressing heavily along the frontiers are the external Germanic peoples who cannot be annihilated or dispersed, but can be managed by a diplomacy whose precondition is the mutual recognition of ultimate Roman military ascendancy. The barbarians may be victorious here or there for a time, but sooner or later the emperor will always assemble enough strength to defeat them, and they know this.

Germanic Infiltration into Roman Leadership

By the end of this period the state of things is quite different. The contingencies of frontier politics—threats, concessions, playing one tribal group off against another—are now being enacted *within* imperial territories. Emperors no longer lead

Roman soldiers attack a German fortress.

armies, but are themselves managed by powerful generals, who are sometimes Germanic tribal leaders as well. No responsible Roman statesman is now so unrealistic as to suppose that Roman armies are any longer dominant. The provinces of the West have identity on paper only. Large Germanic nations in arms are established in Pannonia, Gaul, Spain, Africa, under nominal treaties of alliance, negotiated from a position of Roman weakness. Any serious military undertaking by the imperial government must be indirect, manoeuvring one barbarian people against another. This can still be achieved, but such diplomatic skills cannot compensate for the palpable lack of Roman strength. Imperial laws, symbols, titles and administrative offices continue, but they lack effective coercive power, unless they are vested in warlords who can command the loyalties of the Germanic or Hunnic armies.

We need an adequate understanding of the chain of events in this approximate period, and to distinguish contingent and fortuitous factors from those inherent in the conditions of the time. An immediate search for 'weaknesses' in the empire will not help much, simply because we find too many of them too easily. Weakness is only defined by the scale and likelihood of the task or threat. Every state and empire has many weaknesses, and what is a weakness in one circumstance may be strength in another (the separation of civil and military authority, for example). If a state is unable to survive the combination of every threat on every frontier, every economic disaster and every political crisis erupting simultaneously that is not *weakness*, but rare and senseless misfortune, like the disasters that engulfed Minoan Crete. This is not what happened to the Western Roman empire.

The Roman empire, while retaining a recognisable identity, had succeeded in both absorbing great changes and recovering with great resilience from defeats and disasters. Two large and crude contrasts arise: why was the empire able to resist and survive the great calamities and invasions that so nearly wrecked it in the third century, yet unable to resist similar onslaughts in the fourth and fifth; and why did the Eastern half of the empire ultimately survive, when the Western eventually went under?

In the period in question we can see something of a ratchet effect of declining Roman authority, although it was not of course geographically uniform. At each stage, with each new treaty or bargain on whatever frontier, more concessions have to be made, more frontiers have to be ruthlessly prioritised, and the bargains are correspondingly difficult for the Roman side to enforce. It is not inevitable that the ratchet will move down to the next notch, but stabilisation at each stage becomes increasingly difficult. The margins for manoeuvre and mistake are narrowing. New precedents are already set and cannot be reversed. Once Visigothic *foederati* [federations loyal to Rome] are established and recognised, for example, it is difficult for Theodosius to isolate this treaty settlement as a special and unrepeatable case. Once Alaric combines the office of Roman *Magister* [leader of armies] and Gothic king others will aspire to that position if they are strong enough.

In this discussion we make some use of the word 'inevitable', but not in any interesting sense. There are no strict laws of history—perhaps there are no interesting laws at all. We mean, loosely, that certain kinds of outcome were to be fully expected, given the larger background constraints, irrespective of the fortunes and abilities of individual leaders. Thus, it was inevitable that the impact of Britain's industrial revolution abroad would lead some other nations, such as Germany and the United States, to repeat the process. It was certainly not inevitable that the European tensions and adjustments required by the very rapid growth of Germany should be resolved by war.

It was inevitable that the Roman empire as a whole should be in a virtually permanent emergency over military manpower, and that the armies had to use an ever-increasing proportion of barbarian troops. It was *probably* inevitable that certain kinds of political decision would be taken over the imperial succession, given the very strong nature of dynastic traditions that had been established since Constantine. It was not at all inevitable that Theodosius neglected to train his sons militarily, nor that they should have both turned out to be incapable, nor that Honorius should have lived so long—until 423—under the constant management of military figures that by then the imperial prestige and authority was so disused and ignored that it did not recover.

Most importantly, it was not at all inevitable that the earlier policy of Germanic immigration and recruitment should later have been replaced by *foederati*, Germanic kingdoms and warlords. There is no inexorable continuity from one to another, as Gibbon [the author of *The Decline and Fall of the Roman Empire*] supposed. It is ironic, perhaps, that until very late in the century the Germanic kings did not want to destroy the empire—in the sense of supplanting it with states of their own—they had no such states. What they wanted was settlement land, power and prestige within an imperial framework. Some, such as Athaulf and Wallia, were (in their good moods) decidedly pro-Roman. But, in the process we are describing, successful and enduring treaties and agreements depend less on the attitudes of the parties than on the coincidence of interests and the final constraints of coercive power.

The Hun and Alan migrations into the Danube regions

had disrupted the whole Roman military-diplomatic policy along much of that frontier. This was no longer a simple shift in the tribal power balances as before, which Roman defences and alliances had long been adapted to anticipate and manage. This was a new global situation: the Hun new-comers had rapidly conquered and assimilated parts of the Alan and Gothic nations, and driven the rest to flee from their homelands. These groups no longer had the options of war or peace with Rome, raiding or trade, ransoming pris-oners, renting out warriors and all the other variations of the old chessgame. The Goths had either to acquire territory within the empire, by one means or another, or disappear as an independent people.

New Christian Kingdoms in Western Europe

Jackson Spielvogel

The main Germanic tribes which established kingdoms after the fall of Rome in the west were the Ostrogoths, the Visigoths, the Franks, and the Anglo-Saxons. In this excerpt from his history of western civilization, Jackson Spielvogel suggests that these new Germanic kingdoms represented a combination of both Germanic customs and earlier Roman traditions. Each new kingdom attempted this synthesis in different ways and with varying degrees of success. In addition, in some cases Germanic leaders had to fight or incorporate others, such as the Muslim invaders who arrived in Spain in the eighth century or the resurgent Celts who dominated ancient Britain. Nonetheless, Spielvogel makes clear, the new kingdoms were at least in part a continuation of Rome.

Among the most important aspects of this continuation was the conversion of the Germanic tribes to Christianity. Most adopted Arian Christianity at first, which dominated the Eastern Roman Empire and which claimed that Jesus Christ was human rather than God. Only the Franks took up Roman Catholicism from the beginning. Eventually, however, all the Germans adopted Catholicism as well as the authority of the Pope.

Jackson Spielvogel is associate professor of history at Pennsylvania State University. He is the author of several textbooks as well as the recipient of numerous teaching awards.

By 500, the Western Roman Empire was being replaced politically by a series of kingdoms ruled by German kings. The

Excerpted from J.J. Spielvogel, *Western Civilization Volume A: To 1500, 4th edition*. Copyright © 2000 Wadsworth. Reprinted with permission from Wadsworth, a division of Thomson Learning. Fax 800 730-2215.

pattern of settlement and the fusion of the Romans and Germans took different forms in the various barbarian kingdoms.

The Ostrogothic Kingdom of Italy

More than any other successor state, the Ostrogothic kingdom of Italy managed to maintain the Roman tradition of government. The Ostrogothic king Theodoric had received a Roman education while a hostage in Constantinople. After taking control of Italy, he was eager to create a synthesis of Ostrogothic and Roman practices. In addition to maintaining the entire structure of imperial Roman government, he established separate systems of rule for the Ostrogoths and Romans. The Italian population lived under Roman law administered by Roman officials. The Ostrogoths were governed by their own customs and their own officials. Nevertheless, while the Roman administrative system was kept intact, the Goths alone controlled the army. Despite the apparent success of this "dual approach," Theodoric's system was unable to keep friction from developing between the Italian population and their Germanic overlords.

Religion proved to be a major source of trouble between Ostrogoths and Romans. The Ostrogoths had been converted earlier to Christianity, but to Arian Christianity, and consequently were viewed by the Catholic Italians as heretics. Theodoric's rule grew ever harsher as discontent with Ostrogothic domination deepened. After Theodoric's death in 526, it quickly became apparent that much of his success had been due to the force of his own personality. His successors soon found themselves face-to-face with opposition from the imperial forces of the Byzantine or Eastern Roman Empire. Under Emperor Justinian (527–565), Byzantine armies reconquered Italy between 535 and 552, devastating much of the peninsula and destroying Rome as one of the great urban centers of the Mediterranean world in the process. The Byzantine reconquest proved ephemeral, however. Another German tribe, the Lombards, invaded Italy in 568 and conquered much of northern and central Italy. Unlike the Ostrogoths, the Lombards were harsh rulers and cared little for Roman structures and traditions. The Lombards' fondness for fighting each other enabled the Byzantines to retain control of some parts of Italy, especially the area around Ravenna, which became the capital of imperial government in the west.

The Visigothic Kingdom of Spain

The Visigothic kingdom in Spain, while surviving longer, demonstrated a number of parallels to the Ostrogothic kingdom of Italy. Both favored coexistence between the Roman and German populations; both featured a warrior caste dominating a considerably larger native population; and both inherited and continued to maintain much of the Roman structure of government while largely excluding Romans from power. There were also noticeable differences, however. Perceiving that their Arianism was a stumbling block to good relations, the Visigothic rulers converted to Catholic Christianity in the late sixth century and ended the tension caused by this heresy. Laws preventing intermarriage were dropped, and the Visigothic and Hispano-Roman peoples began to fuse together. A new body of law common to both peoples also developed.

The kingdom possessed one fatal weakness, however—the Visigoths fought constantly over the kingship. The Visigoths had no law of hereditary kingship and no established procedure for choosing new rulers. Church officials tried to help develop a sense of order, as this canon from the Fourth Council of Toledo in 633 illustrates: "No one of us shall dare to seize the kingdom; no one shall arouse sedition among the citizenry; no one shall think of killing the king. . . ." Church decrees failed to stop the feuds, however, and assassinations remained a way of life in Visigothic Spain. In 711, Muslim invaders destroyed the Visigothic kingdom itself.

The Frankish Kingdom

Only one of the German kingdoms on the European continent proved long-lasting—the kingdom of the Franks. The establishment of a Frankish kingdom was the work of Clovis (c. 482–511), the leader of one group of Franks who eventually became king of them all.

It is highly significant that Clovis became a Catholic Christian around 500. Unlike many other Germanic peoples who converted first to Arian Christianity, Clovis converted from paganism directly to Catholic Christianity, a move that furthered the development of a society based on the fusion of Gallo-Romans and Germans. Clovis's action had other repercussions as well. He gained the support of the western church and the Roman popes who were only too eager to obtain the friendship of a major Germanic ruler who was a Catholic Christian. The conversion of the king also paved the way for the conversion of the Frankish peoples. Finally, Clovis could justify his expansionary tendencies at the beginning of the sixth century by posing as a defender of the orthodox Christian faith. He defeated the Alemanni in southwest Germany and the Visigoths in southern Gaul. By 510, Clovis had established a powerful new Frankish kingdom stretching from the Pyrenees in the west to the German lands in the east.

To control his new kingdom, Clovis came to rely on his Frankish followers who ruled in the old Roman city-states under the title of "count." Often these officials were forced to share power with the Gallo-Roman Catholic bishops, producing a gradual fusion of Latin and German cultures with the church serving to preserve the Latin culture. Clovis was also responsible for establishing the Merovingian dynasty, a name derived from Merovech, their semi-legendary ancestor. Clovis spent the last years of his life ensuring the survival of his dynasty by killing off relatives who were leaders of other groups of Franks.

After the death of Clovis, his sons divided the newly created kingdom. During the sixth and seventh centuries, the once-united Frankish kingdom came to be partitioned into three major areas: Neustria in northern Gaul; Austrasia, consisting of the ancient Frankish lands on both sides of the Rhine; and the former kingdom of Burgundy. All three were ruled by members of the Merovingian dynasty. Within the three territories, the Merovingian kings were assisted by powerful nobles. Frankish society possessed a ruling class that gradually intermarried with the old Gallo-

Roman senatorial class to form a new nobility. These noble families took advantage of their position to strengthen their own lands and wealth at the expense of the monarchy. Within the royal household, the position of *major domus* or mayor of the palace, the chief officer of the king's household, began to overshadow the king. Essentially, both nobles and mayors of the palace were expanding their power at the expense of the kings.

At the beginning of the eighth century, the most important political development in the Frankish kingdom was the rise of Charles Martel, who served as mayor of the palace of Austrasia beginning in 714. Charles Martel defeated the Muslims near Poitiers in 732 and by the time of his death in 741 had become virtual ruler of the three Merovingian kingdoms. Though he was not king, Charles Martel's dynamic efforts put his family on the verge of creating a new dynasty that would establish an even more powerful Frankish state.

During the sixth and seventh centuries, the Frankish kingdom witnessed a process of fusion between Gallo-Roman and Frankish cultures and peoples, a process accompanied by a significant decline in Roman standards of civilization and commercial activity. The Franks were warriors and did little to encourage either urban life or trade. Commerce declined in the interior, though seacoast towns maintained some activity. By 750, Frankish Gaul was basically an agricultural society in which the old Roman *latifundia* system of the late empire had continued unimpeded. Institutionally, however, Germanic concepts of kingship and customary law had replaced the Roman governmental structure.

Anglo-Saxon England

The barbarian pressures on the Western Roman Empire had forced the emperors to withdraw the Roman armies and abandon Britain by the beginning of the fifth century. This opened the door to the Angles and Saxons, Germanic tribes from Denmark and northern Germany. Although these same peoples had made plundering raids for the past century, the withdrawal of the Roman armies enabled them to make settlements instead. They met with resistance from the

Celtic Britons, however, who still controlled the western regions of Cornwall, Wales, and Cumberland at the beginning of the seventh century. The German invaders eventually succeeded in carving out small kingdoms throughout the island, Kent in southeast England being one of them. This wave of German invaders would eventually be converted to Christianity by new groups of Christian missionaries.

Chapter 3

The Byzantine Empire and Eastern Orthodox Christianity

Turning|Points

IN WORLD HISTORY

The Emergence of the Byzantine Empire

J.M. Hussey

Christianity had become a major religion in the eastern part of the Roman Empire by the time Constantine became emperor in 306. Partly in recognition of the new religion, Constantine selected a new Roman capital at a Greek city known as Byzantium. The site, which was later renamed Constantinople, had other advantages besides its proximity to Christian activity. It was far away from the Germanic tribes of the west, and it stood astride traditional routes of trade and travel.

In the following selection, J.M. Hussey asserts that the Byzantine Empire, as it was to be called after the fall of the west, grew smoothly out of the Roman Empire. No distinct break took place. Only after the Germanic tribes had overrun the west did the Byzantine Empire achieve a unique identity. It was, Hussey claims, oriented to what we call today the Middle East. Those areas were wealthier than Europe, most Christian activity and controversy took place there, and finally, the east was where the "Romans," as they still considered themselves, found new military challenges.

J.M. Hussey was a professor of history at the University of London.

In 324 Byzantium, the old Greek settlement in the triangle of land bordered by the waters of the Golden Horn, the Bosphorus and the Sea of Marmora, was chosen by the Roman Emperor Constantine the Great as the site for a new city to be the headquarters of the Empire in the East.

It was formally inaugurated in May 330 as the City of Constantine, his residence and one of the capitals. Various eastern centres had previously been tried out but this proved permanent and was indeed, by its geographical situation, admirably suited to serve as a link between Europe and Asia, between the Black Sea with its unexploited hinterland and the Aegean and Mediterranean Seas opening on the routes to the Middle and Far East. The very foundation of an eastern capital, the seat of the senior Emperor, pointed the way to the middle ages when it was the eastern half of the Roman Empire which survived without any break in its history. It is immaterial whether it is called early Byzantine or late Roman during this formative period inaugurated by Constantine the Great. It was essentially the Roman Empire and as such its culture was predominantly Greek, though with strong oriental influences. This was true of the Roman Empire in the days of St. Paul as in the days of St. Ambrose. The difference between the world of Paul of Tarsus and of Ambrose of Milan lay however not in the structure of the imperial framework or the nature of Graeco-Roman civilization, but in two fundamental changes. Internally, increasing concern with the East and with its creeds was symbolized by the New Rome which rose on the shores of the Bosphorus, the city of the first Christian Emperor. Externally, the dangerous pressure of a rival Empire in Persia and the even more threatening menace of migratory tribes from the North weakened imperial resources, and though warded off in the East, eventually brought about the political disruption of the western half of the Roman Empire and the rise of new independent principalities under the control of the Germanic invaders.

The Emperor Constantine Accepts Christianity

In Constantine the Great's day the imminent disruption of the western half of the Roman Empire was however not yet apparent. What must have caused some stir was the Emperor's announcement of his adoption of Christianity and the toleration and favour henceforth accorded the Christian Church, a toleration which by the end of the fourth century had been replaced by its recognition as the one true faith and the consequent proscription of all other religions. Pagan practices were by no means thus eliminated and lingered on for many generations and even centuries, but it was useless to plead for toleration or to claim that not by one road alone could so great a truth be reached. Whatever the nature of the 'conversion' which Constantine experienced, his belief in the Christian God and his Roman heritage convinced him of his duty to take the lead in promoting doctrinal and disciplinary unity within the Christian Church. He called and presided over the first General Council of the Church at Nicaea (325). He thus personified the close understanding between Church and State which marked the medieval East Roman Empire. His historian, Bishop Eusebius, laid the foundations of a theory of Christian sovereignty, emphasizing, not the cleavage between the two cities or between what was God's and what was Caesar's, but the Christian Empire, temporal it is true, but sanctified as a divine instrument and ruled over by an Emperor who was Christ's vicegerent on earth. The titles of 'thirteenth apostle' and 'the equal of the apostles' fitly recognize the place of Constantine the Great in the medieval polity.

In many respects the Empire in the fourth century shows no abrupt break with the earlier period; it might just as well be called late Roman as early Byzantine. It showed its close cultural affinities with the Hellenistic world, and the adoption of Christianity did not mean the rejection of pagan civilization: the learning, art, philosophy of Greece remained the prized possessions of a Christian Byzantium. Its government was in essence that of the Graeco-Roman Empire. It continued to be ruled by a single absolute monarch, whose authority was enhanced by his special position as the chosen representative of the Christian God. . . .

Military need was indeed the keynote of the early Byzantine state. The army, itself often recruited and officered by Germanic elements, was continually called upon to drive back the barbarians on the north, or to face pressure on the east from the vigorous Persian King of kings. It was partly because the Danube and the eastern frontiers were obvious danger spots that Constantine (like Diocletian before him) had chosen to take over the eastern half of the Empire himself, while his colleague ruled in the West. The weight of the Empire was in the East: the *pars orientalis* [eastern lands] was wealthier with greater economic resources, more densely populated, the home of fertile intellectual and religious activity, and its great cities, such as the cosmopolitan Alexandria or Antioch, or even the newly founded but rapidly growing imperial city on the Bosphorus, could rival Rome.

The Roman Empire Begins to Split into Eastern and Western Halves

In the late third and throughout the fourth centuries various methods of ruling the Empire were tried, ranging from control by a single Emperor alone to the more elaborate government by four which Diocletian devised. Though there might be one or more assistant Emperors it was emphasized that the Empire remained one and indivisible. All the same the eastern and western halves were growing apart and had different political problems.

In 395, the Emperor Theodosius the Great died and left the eastern half to Arcadius his elder son, the western to the younger Honorius. The indivisibility of the Empire was still maintained. For instance, laws issued for one half were valid if proclaimed in the other half. But political events shattered Roman rule in the West. From the end of the fourth century up to Justinian's reign in the mid-sixth century the West (i.e. the prefectures of Italy and the Gauls) lacked capable Emperors. Collapse in the face of barbarian pressure was averted only by the ability of the generals who took control, themselves often of Germanic origin, such as Stilicho or Ricimer.

The Germanic migratory tribes had long caused grave anxiety to the Empire and were shortly to transform the western provinces from distant Britain to Italy and North Africa. Nor did the East escape unscathed. In the late fourth century the Goths who had been harassing the frontiers poured into the Balkans and crushingly defeated the Roman army in 378. Theodosius the Great and later Emperors tried to deal with this problem in various ways. Many of the Goths settled in the Balkans and were recognized as a kind of military auxiliary force (*foederati*) in the pay of the Emperor, a costly proceeding. They proved a disturbing element, plundering the Balkans and Greece at will and influencing politics, so that the government in Constantinople was only too relieved when they were diverted elsewhere. The Visigoths after sacking Rome in 410 passed to South France and Spain. Later in the century the Emperor Zeno was thankful to send a substantial number of them to Italy, where they went in 488, men, women and children, under the leadership of Theodoric the Ostrogoth.

Italy by the end of the fifth century, like most of the western provinces, was virtually lost to the Empire. The line of Roman Emperors, the descendants of Theodosius the Great, had been replaced by leaders of Germanic origin, and control of the peninsula was in the hands of Odoacer. Theodoric the Ostrogoth however succeeded in establishing himself not as Emperor, nor as an independent ruler, such as his contemporary Clovis in France, but as the representative of the Roman Emperor in Constantinople. So well did he rule that he did indeed deserve to be called a 'righteous Emperor', said his younger contemporary Procopius writing in the sixth century.

While Italy and the West were in the hands of these new settlers, the East was more fortunate. The successful reign of Theodosius II (408–450) with its care for learning and foundation of the university, its sound administration, its extension of the city boundaries and erection of the massive fortified walls on the land side of Constantinople, was in contrast to the less happy fate of the sister capital of Rome.

The Early Byzantine Empire Faced Military and Religious Challenges

But the eastern half of the Empire was not without its difficulties. It looked at one point in the later fifth century as though the Germanic element, already present in some strength within the Empire both as settlers and as soldiers, would dominate the imperial government itself, as was already happening at Rome; but again large numbers were diverted to the West. More important still, the East could draw on its own native highlands of Asia Minor both for soldiers and for leaders, who successfully countered the German Aspar and his followers. Asia Minor now, as later, proved a tower of strength to the Empire.

The real problems of the East were of another nature. The vigorous Sassanian Empire lay hard by its eastern reaches. Both powers coveted the strategic Caucasian area and manœuvred for allies in these regions. Both sought to maintain a measure of control in the desert country bordering on the Roman provinces of Syria, Palestine and Egypt. Perpetual vigilance and frequent conflict marked relations between Persian and Roman on the eastern frontiers, but to the Romans the Persians were a very different foe from the barbarians who flooded into the Empire. They had a tradition and a civilization comparable to that of the Graeco-Roman world. In the late sixth century the Roman historian Theophylact Simocattes could write, 'From the very beginning Divine Providence caused the whole world to be illuminated by two eyes from above, that is, by the most powerful kingdom of the Romans and by the most wise sceptres of the Persian polity.'

Even more serious than the ambitions of the militant Persian Empire was the acute discontent within the eastern provinces. Growing resentment at Roman rule was particularly marked in Syria, Palestine and Egypt and was fundamentally due to local consciousness of an affinity with an oriental and not a western, or Graeco-Roman, way of life. This separatism was shown in various ways, such as the development of national languages and literature, which appear side by side with the international medium Greek. In Egypt the native language, Coptic, was widely used for everyday purposes and was often the only language understood or read. In large monasteries where there were probably both Greek and Coptic speaking monks and where many visitors from the Mediterranean world might be expected, there would be interpreters. Differences of language, custom and idiom, as well as political antagonisms, were sharply reflected in religious problems from the fourth century onwards. The first General Church Council in 325 had been called by Constantine the Great to discuss and pronounce upon questions of doctrine and organization. This conciliar method, though not the only way of settling ecclesiastical difficulties, was widely followed throughout the middle ages. The Christian Church, when it received imperial recognition in 313, was already well organized. The lead was taken by the bishops of the great centres of Rome, Antioch and Alexandria, and in the course of the fourth century Constantinople rapidly secured a place for itself in the first rank. In the General Council of Constantinople of 381, and again at Chalcedon in 451, it was recognized that the see of St. Peter had primacy of honour, but so rapidly had Constantinople grown in prestige and importance that it now ousted Alexandria and Antioch and took the second place. 'The bishop of Constantinople shall have the primacy of honour after the bishop of Rome, because the same is New Rome' (Council of Constantinople 381, canon 3), which was a bitter blow to the Patriarchs of Alexandria, 'the uncrowned kings of Roman Egypt'.

As Constantine the Great had found, it was by no means easy to inculcate harmony and unity into the Christian Church. Many still followed one or other of the pagan religions, and many were sceptical of any religion at all. The Church had to face the renewed attack of clear-headed and able thinkers, and partly for this reason, partly in response to its own teaching needs, it had to articulate and define its doctrine. The centre of its teaching was the Christian God, and the Church met its greatest difficulties when it attempted to define the nature of God. In stormy meetings of the councils the bishops, most of them from the eastern sees, for in comparison the West was as yet less populated and less well organized, hammered out for the guidance of their own and future generations the definitions of the Trinity and particularly of its Second Person, God the Son. The age-long antagonisms of the great ecclesiastical centres, rising political hatred, and even personal rivalries resulted in turbulence and bitter dissension. But Bibles hurled at opponents and the vivid recording of beards plucked out and fractured limbs, must not obscure the constructive work of these churchmen. Their precise formulation of Christian doctrine laid the foundations on which Christian teaching and theology still build today.

The Emperor Justinian I

Donald M. Nicol

After the Western Roman Empire was dismembered by Germanic tribes, the Roman tradition was maintained in the east. The Eastern Roman Empire is also known as the Byzantine Empire, named after its capital, a Greek city called Byzantium. The city of Byzantium itself received a new name: Constantinople.

In the following selection, Donald M. Nicol describes how one of the early Byzantine emperors, Justinian I, tried to keep alive the traditions of Rome. He thought of the empire as a single entity, united by the Christian religion and by the person of the emperor. His efforts to revive the empire included brief military conquests of the Germanic tribes in Italy and North Africa.

More importantly, however, Justinian was willing to adapt Roman traditions to fit the new realities of an empire that was largely Greek-speaking. According to Nicol, the greatest of his legacies was his collection of Roman law, written in Latin but amended in Greek. This collection, the *Codex Justinianus* or Justinian's Code, kept Roman law alive for centuries.

Donald M. Nicol was professor of Byzantine and modern Greek Studies at King's College, University of London.

When Constantine became sole ruler of the Roman Empire he was still a pagan. Though Rome was now a monarchy, daily life continued to conform to customs which had become established in the days of the Republic. Constantine's assumption of supreme power was therefore not confirmed by means of a coronation service of the type which was to become usual in feudal times in Europe. Instead it was rati-

Excerpted from Donald M. Nicol, "Justinian I and His Successors," in *Byzantium: An Introduction*, edited by Philip Whitting. Copyright © Philip Whitting. Reprinted with permission from St. Martin's Press, LLC.

fied by a ceremony which dated back to the days when Rome's caesar was elected to the highest office in the Empire by his fellow-citizens. In accordance with that ancient custom Constantine was placed on a shield and lifted up on it in full view of his army and the assembled people. Their cheers sufficed to establish him in his new position. That method of informing the nation of the elevation of a new sovereign to the Empire's throne persisted in Byzantium during the best part of 100 years, the first rulers to succeed Constantine being presented to the assembled Senate, army and people of Constantinople in the same manner as Rome's caesars. Like them, they received from the hands of an eminent official the coronet which served as the emperor's emblem of office. However, by the year 457 when Leo I came to the throne, the patriarch [the head of the Eastern Christian Church] of Constantinople had become so important in the state that his authority almost equalled that of the emperor and it therefore fell to him in preference to a layman, however distinguished, to place the crown on Leo's head. Leo's immediate successors decided to be similarly crowned by the patriarchs of their day, with the result that from Justinian's time onwards the ceremony was always performed in the capital's principal church, the great cathedral of Haghia Sophia. The original structure begun by Constantine I had been destroyed in the Nika riots in 532, but it was rebuilt on a grander scale by Justinian.

Crowning the Byzantine Emperors

Over the years, coronations were celebrated in Byzantium with ever-increasing pomp and magnificence. By the tenth century the ritual had become so elaborate that Emperor Constantine VII Porphyrogenitus (913–59) thought that it would prove helpful to his son and heir if he recorded it in detail in a book he was engaged in writing for the boy's use later in life. It was called *The Book of Ceremonies;* the description of the coronation occupies several pages, for the emperor listed in full the part played by all officials, senators and members of the factions, their precise positions in the official procession, the clothes each wore and the badges of

Emperor Justinian I (center) with his bodyguards, ministers, and Bishop Maximian of Ravenna (third from right).

office they carried. Thus patricians were to appear in white *chlamydes* or cloaks trimmed with gold.

On entering the cathedral the sovereign was met by the patriarch, who assisted him in changing his robes for some which were believed to have been given to Constantine the Great by angels, and which were therefore carefully kept in the cathedral for use by the emperor only on certain specific occasions. Then the patriarch took the emperor by the hand to lead him into the body of the great church. On reaching the silver gates the emperor lit the special candles reserved for his use and moved to a porphyry slab set into the floor in front of the royal gates of the *iconostasis* (an altar screen designed to display icons) to pray. Only then, accompanied by the patriarch, did he penetrate beyond the *iconostasis* to enter the altar enclosure. This procedure was followed whenever the emperor attended a religious ceremony in the cathedral—it is estimated that his presence there was required on an average some 30 times a month. The patriarch always conducted the religious service which followed, in the case of a coronation reading a prayer over the crown before placing it on the emperor's head amidst the acclamations of the assembled worshippers. The emperor then moved to the throne, often one made of gold, which had been placed in the *mitato-*

rion (throne room). When he was seated all the assembled people, following a strict order of precedence, passed before him, paying homage by prostrating themselves before him.

An Emperor Chosen by God

By the ninth century the habit of crowning an emperor during a religious ceremony had become so firmly established that it was henceforth observed by all other Christian monarchs. However, in Byzantium it also remained necessary for the emperor to sign a profession of faith before he was crowned. From the start the crowning of an emperor by a patriarch was regarded throughout Byzantium as an act of outstanding significance, being interpreted as the visual confirmation of the belief that the emperor was God's chosen representative on earth. As such, emperors were soon being revered almost as sacred personages. In art they were sometimes represented wearing a halo; in conversation and literature they were often compared to the apostles, and a ruler was even occasionally described as the 'thirteenth apostle' and his residences as 'sacred palaces'. An emperor's semicelestial nature was reflected in his use of an immensely wide throne. In reality it was a double throne, which enabled the pagan custom of the partially empty throne to be retained and adapted to Christian observances: henceforth, the right side of such thrones was dedicated to Christ, and to make this visibly apparent a copy of the Gospels was placed on it. It remained vacant on Sundays and during religious festivals, when the emperor occupied the left side of the throne. On working days, on the other hand, the emperor, acting as Christ's representative on earth, used the right half, doing the same on all state occasions as well as when granting audiences to visiting ambassadors.

When the emperor appeared in the streets of his cities, the crowds often acclaimed him as God's representative, and as he advanced hymns to that effect were sung by choirs, the members of which were drawn from the city's political guildsmen and factions. Candles, torches and incense were carried before the emperor as they were before the holy icons and prelates in religious processions. Even inefficient

A Visit to the Byzantine Emperor

Liudprand, a bishop from Italy, made a visit to Constantinople in 949. In his chronicle, he noted the impressiveness of the emperor and his court.

Before the emperor's seat stood a tree, made of bronze gilded over, whose branches were filled with birds, also made of gilded bronze, which uttered different cries, each according to its varying species. The throne itself was so marvellously fashioned that at one moment it seemed a low structure, and at another it rose high into the air. It was of immense size and was guarded by lions, made either of bronze or of wood covered with gold, who beat the ground with their tails and gave a dreadful roar with open mouth and quivering tongue. Leaning upon the shoulders of two eunuchs I was brought into the emperor's presence. At my approach the lions began to roar and the birds to cry out, each according to its kind; but I was neither terrified nor surprised, for I had previously made enquiry about all these things from people who were well acquainted with them. So after I had three times made obeisance to the emperor with my face upon the ground, I lifted my head, and behold! the man whom just before I had seen sitting on a moderately elevated seat had now changed his raiment and was sitting on the level of the ceiling. How it was done I could not imagine, unless perhaps he was lifted up by some such sort of device as we use for raising the timbers of a wine press. On that occasion he did not address me personally, since even if he had wished to do so the wide distance between us would have rendered conversation unseemly, but by the intermediary of a secretary he enquired about Berengar's doings and asked after his health. I made a fitting reply and then, at a nod from the interpreter, left his presence and retired to my lodging.

Selection from *The Works of Liudprand of Cremona*, translated by Frederick Adam Wright. Reprinted by permission of E.P. Dutton and Co., and Routledge and Kegan Paul Ltd. in *The Early Middle Ages, 500–100*, ed. Robert Brentano. New York: Free Press, 1964.

and bad rulers—of whom Byzantium had more than her fair share—were thought to have been raised to their exalted position by the Almighty, who had selected them for their high office for the purpose of testing the faithful.

The Roman conception of an elected ruler, whether acting as the head of state or as emperor, was so firmly embedded in the Roman mind that, in Byzantium, the office of emperor was not at first regarded as hereditary. When time and events permitted it was therefore considered right for a dying or ageing ruler to choose his successor. In the event of an emperor's sudden death the members of his immediate family were entitled to select the new ruler, but if the dead man had no close relatives or if, as often happened, his rule had been brought to an end as the result of a revolution, it then fell to the Senate to make the appointment. Justinian, perhaps the greatest of all the Byzantine emperors, came to the throne in that manner. No significance was attached to ancient lineage, and class distinctions were considered of so little importance that the fact that Justin (518–27) was by birth a Macedonian peasant did not prevent him from occupying the throne for nine years. . . .

By the seventh century it had become the custom for the emperors to choose one of their sons, not necessarily the elder, to succeed them. First they waited to appoint him till they were well on in life or until they thought that death was drawing near, but before long they found it wiser to ensure the survival of their dynasty and to guard against sudden death by choosing their heir early in their reigns, and for similar reasons they gradually started selecting two sons for the office, naming them in order of preference. These appointments were legalised by a religious ceremony conducted on very much the same lines as an emperor's coronation. (There were two minor differences: the coronation was held in one of the palace churches instead of in the cathedral of Hagia Sophia and, after blessing their crowns, the patriarch passed them to the emperor who, as in the case of his wife's coronation, personally placed them on the heads of his co-rulers.) The senior and favourite co-ruler gradually came to be spoken of as 'the little *basileus*' and his picture often appeared beside his father's on the country's coinage. . . .

Emperors Were "Born in the Purple"

As soon as it became possible for them to do so the emperors naturally chose one of their sons to succeed them, and so the office of sovereign gradually came to be accepted as a hereditary one. But because the emperors were not obliged to appoint their eldest son to succeed them, gradually particular importance was attached to the children who were born to a reigning couple. Such children were born in the Purple Bedchamber in the Purple Palace—a residence which owed its name to the fact that the walls of the empress's bedchamber were hung with stuff, generally silk, the colour of porphyry. Though a very small number of senior court officials were allowed to wear purple cloaks, stuffs of that colour were reserved for the exclusive use of members of the imperial family. They alone could wear purple-coloured robes and shoes, and be buried in porphyry sarcophagi. Children born in the Purple Bedchamber in the Purple Palace automatically received the appellation of Porphyrogenitus, meaning 'born in the purple'—an expression which lives on in our own language and times—and, in the case of boys, this lucky occurrence increased their chances of inheriting the crown. Such princes were surrounded by every conceivable luxury. Inevitably, when it eventually became customary for the first-born of these sons to succeed his father, rivalry broke out between him and his brothers, some of them his elders. It was made all the fiercer by the fact that an emperor's sons were often no more than half-brothers, their father having married more than once. Many an heir to supreme power ended his days in prison, in solitary confinement, having first had to submit to tortures which included blinding, having his tongue or nose cut off, or even worse. A deposed brother who was allowed to withdraw for ever to a remote monastery, to become a monk and spend his days in prayer and contemplation, was to be counted fortunate.

Byzantine Women Could Become Powerful

Imperial weddings were accompanied by an extremely solemn, elaborate and magnificent ritual. All wore their finest clothes and official robes for the occasion. The imperial bridal couple appeared wearing their imperial crowns below the wedding crowns which are still used at Orthodox weddings. But whereas today the wedding crowns are held above the heads of the groom and bride, throughout the religious ceremony in Byzantium a sumptuous purple-coloured fabric was suspended above the heads of the imperial couple. The patriarch performed the marriage ceremony; after it all those who had attended the wedding, patricians and eminent officials, were expected to prostrate themselves before the bridal couple. Then they formed themselves into a procession and accompanied their newly wedded sovereigns to the Magnaura Palace where the choirs of the Blue and Green factions were waiting to welcome them by singing to the accompaniment of an organ belonging to the Green faction. The bridal couple then proceeded to their bridal chamber still wearing their crowns; there they received their guests and in their presence they removed their crowns, placing them on their bridal bed. Then all went to the Dining Hall of the Nineteen Couches where, changing into simpler garments, the emperor and empress sat down to their wedding breakfast with their guests. On such occasions women were included in the party, but they were not permitted to dress their hair in the high style known as the *propoloma*. Generally, however, the empresses, many of whom possessed large fortunes, and all of whom were waited upon by numerous courtiers and retainers, entertained the eminent women of Byzantium at sumptuous banquets held in their own apartments.

Women were not quite so free in Byzantium as they had been in Rome, where they were generally treated as the equals of men. In Byzantium, though empresses took part in many aspects of public life, they were nevertheless expected to spend much of their time in the women's quarters. Like women of lower station, many must have used much of their leisure, if not weaving like their humbler subjects, then at any rate in doing fine embroidery as adornments for their favourite churches. Time and again empresses and other women greatly influenced public events and were often the dominating members of their family circle. Many an empress became a powerful autocrat, even to the extent of ruling at times in her own right. At certain periods of Byzantine history, and more especially during the opening phase (when members both of Rome's ancient aristocracy and of Greece's nobility were establishing the standards and conventions which were to characterise Byzantium) empresses were chosen regardless of rank and origin from among the Empire's most beautiful girls. In contrast to office, birth counted for astonishingly little in Byzantium.

The Political Accomplishments of Justinian I

Tamara Talbot Rice

In 324, the Roman Emperor Constantine surprised his many subjects when he announced that he was transferring the capital of the Roman Empire to Byzantium, a small town in the Greek-speaking east. Among the advantages that Byzantium held, according to Constantine, was its access to trade and communication routes. Moreover, Byzantium was nearer than Rome to the early centers of Christianity. Byzantium soon became known as Constantinople; today it is the city of Istanbul in Turkey. Constantine, for his part, was the first Roman emperor to convert to Christianity.

In the following selection from her history of daily life in the eastern Roman, or Byzantine, empire, Tamara Talbot Rice describes the extravagant nature of life around the emperors. They lived in great luxury and were crowned in elaborate ceremonies. Emperors were even accorded religious significance; they were considered God's representatives on earth. As Rice points out, however, Byzantine power was not always straightforward; heirs were not always eldest sons, and empresses and noblewomen often exercised influence behind the throne.

Tamara Talbot Rice is the author of many books on Byzantine, Near Eastern, and Russian history and art, including *Icons*, *The Scythians*, and *A Concise History of Russian Art*.

The rulers of the Roman Empire, holding absolute authority over so large a part of the world, were sometimes able to shape the destiny of a whole generation or an age. The age of Justinian covered most of the sixth century. Some have called it the last century of the Roman Empire. For it was Justinian who made the last successful attempt to reunite under the rule of one man all the provinces of ancient Rome, to reconstitute the undivided and universal Empire of Augustus and the Caesars.

In the century before, most of the western part of that Empire had been lost. The Ostrogoths had established a kingdom in Italy, the Visigoths in Spain, and the Vandals in North Africa. On the eastern frontier lay the Sassanid Empire of the Persians, a greater rival to the power of Rome than any barbarian kingdom. But the Persians were a perennial and familiar problem; and the land that they occupied had never been Roman. To Justinian, and to many of his contemporaries, it was the recovery of the lost western provinces which was the obvious duty of a true Roman Emperor. And most of his reign was directed to this end.

Justinian succeeded his uncle Justin I in 527. He was already forty-five and his views on imperial policy were formed. His appearance is plain for all to see in the mosaic portraits of him in the churches at Ravenna, or in the magnificent gold and copper coins of his reign. But his character has been for ever distorted by the poison pen of the great Greek historian of the age, Procopius of Caesarea. Procopius composed a history of Justinian's wars against the Vandals, Goths and Persians, and also a flattering account of the Emperor's building works. But, for reasons best known to himself, and strictly for private consumption, he also wrote a Secret History, in which Justinian and his wife, the famous Theodora, are lampooned as monsters of wickedness and deceit. Reading between the lines of Procopius, however, one can discern in Justinian a man strong-willed when fortune favoured him, though hesitant in time of crisis; a religious fanatic but with some of the qualities of a monk; a restless person and yet a tireless, dedicated ruler. Even Procopius admired the Emperor's ascetic nature, misdirected though his mortifications might be. These are his words:

'As a general rule he cared little for sleep, and never overindulged in food or drink, but picked at the food with his fingers before going away. For he regarded such things as a kind of irrelevancy necessitated by nature. He would often fast for two days and nights at a time, especially during Lent, or live on wild herbs and water. He would sleep for not more than an hour and then spend the rest of the night pacing up and down. For he made it his business to be constantly vigilant, suffering and striving for the sole purpose of bringing a continuous, daily sequence of disasters upon his subjects.'

The Influence of Theodora

Theodora, the belly-dancer whom Justinian defied convention to marry, fares even worse at the hands of Procopius. But it is clear that she was possessed of no ordinary beauty, charm and intelligence. She was a born actress and enjoyed being the centre of attraction as the great lady of the imperial court; and in contrast to her austere husband she revelled in the luxury, pomp and elegance of life in the Great Palace at Constantinople. She shared to the full his conception of the majesty of the Roman Empire. But whereas Justinian belonged to the Latin world and thought like a Roman, Theodora was a Greek or perhaps one may say a Byzantine. Their views on many subjects differed. But as man and wife they complemented one another. Justinian was devoted to her, and her death in 548 marked a turning-point in his career.

The age of Justinian was called into being by a number of variously gifted men, who translated the Emperor's dreams into reality. There was the administrator John of Cappadocia, who became Prefect of the City, a man utterly without scruples and deservedly hated, not least by Theodora, who finally secured his disgrace. It was he who raised the taxes to pay for Justinian's ambitious schemes. There was Tribonian the lawyer, the main author of the great compilation of Roman law that Justinian commissioned. There were the generals Belisarius and Narses, fighting on all the frontiers from Syria to Italy. There were the scientists Anthemius of Tralles and Isidore of Miletus, the architects of the church of the Holy Wisdom. But the greatness of the age of itself inspired creative activity of all kinds, in poetry, painting, theology, science, medicine and the writing of history. Agathias continued the history of Procopius, but also wrote poetry and published a well-known Anthology. Romanus Melodus set the standard of Byzantine hymn-writing for the future; and a merchant seaman called Cosmas Indicopleustes related his travels to the shape and structure of the universe as he conceived it.

Justinian the Autocrat

The inhabited part of that structure was the ecumenical or universal Christian Roman Empire whose citizens obeyed one law and professed one creed. This was the ideal before Justinian's mind. He had a passion for imposing uniformity on his heterogeneous subjects whether they wished it or not. For he was convinced that he, better than they, knew God's plan for the order of the world and was indeed God's agent for the fulfilment of that plan. Those of his subjects in Constantinople who opposed his autocratic policy were taught a bitter lesson early in his reign. The opposition showed itself in a riot that broke out in the Hippodrome in 532. Much of the city was burnt by the mob, and some of the senators proclaimed a rival Emperor. Justinian lost his nerve and would have run away, had not Theodora shamed him into action. The imperial troops were turned on the rioters, and 30,000 people were massacred in the Hippodrome.

The 'Nika riot', as it is called, was the crisis of Justinian's career. Thereafter he was not troubled by political opponents. In the same year 532, after five years of border warfare, he made a treaty of peace with the king of the Persians. Many of the troops engaged in holding the eastern frontier could now be redeployed for the rescue of the western provinces. It is tempting to picture Justinian as the mastermind directing a well-planned campaign of reconquest from his headquarters in Constantinople. But in fact the work was done piece-meal, as the opportunities presented themselves. It began with the recovery of North Africa from the Vandals. Belisarius commanded the armada that set out in June 533.

It was blessed by the Patriarch of Constantinople, for this was a just and holy war to liberate a Roman province from the oppression of an alien tyrant who was also, and this was worse, a heretic. The Vandal kingdom was destroyed within the year; its king Gelimer surrendered in March 534. Guerrilla warfare went on in North Africa for another fifteen years, but it was against the Berber natives and not against usurping aliens. For a lost province of the Empire had been restored to Roman rule.

The Reconquest of Italy

The opportunity to intervene in Sicily and Italy arose in 535 when the Gothic queen Amalasuntha was murdered by her cousin Theodahad. Amalasuntha had been the friend and ally of the Roman Empire. But the Goths, like the Vandals, were Arian heretics. The salvation of the souls of the Italians, as well as their political welfare, demanded their liberation from Gothic rule. Once again the commander of the enterprise was Belisarius. In June 535 he took a fleet to Sicily, while an army marched overland into Dalmatia. Sicily fell within a few months, and on the last day of the year Belisarius entered Syracuse.

It really seemed as if divine favour smiled on Justinian's armies. . . .

By 555 Justinian could boast that the Mediterranean was once again a Roman lake. In the reconquered territories the old Roman provincial administration was reimposed as though there had been no change in circumstances. Sicily was placed under the rule of a praetor. Sardinia and Corsica came under the viceroy of North Africa. Italy was reconstituted as a province, governed by a Prefect with his headquarters at Ravenna; and an inscription set into a bridge over the Anio river proclaimed to the bewildered Romans that their former happiness had now been restored to them.

To many in the West, who had come to regard the Gothic régime as permanent and now found it swept away by the horrors of a war of liberation, the imperial propaganda from faraway Constantinople must have sounded hollow. In the eastern provinces, however, things were different. For until the recent invasion of Syria by the Persians the great cities of the eastern Mediterranean had continued to enjoy the security, if not the happiness, provided by the Roman Empire. Their inhabitants had not been required to adjust themselves to the collapse of their world and to the indignities of a non-Roman régime. They were accustomed to prosperity and to a high standard of living. The wealthy and sophisticated aristocracy of Constantinople expected to be provided with a steady flow of luxury goods from the far east; and Justinian did not disappoint them. The normal trade routes to India and China ran along the caravan trails through Persia, or by sea through the Indian Ocean. But the Persian Wars interrupted this traffic. Justinian therefore explored the alternative routes, by way of the Red Sea and overland by way of the Crimea, where Greek merchants already had well-established markets. But neither alternative was wholly satisfactory. The problem was partly solved when two monks, who had lived in China and there learnt the art of the manufacture of silk, were persuaded to smuggle some silk worms' eggs to Constantinople. Thenceforth, though it took many years to develop, the silk industry became one of the most flourishing and lucrative state monopolies in the Byzantine Empire.

Justinian's Adaptation of Roman Law

The hope that the world had returned to the old order of the Roman Empire was fostered by Justinian's revision of the imperial laws. The Codex Justinianus, compiled by Tribonian and a legal commission in 529, contained all the valid edicts of the Emperors since the time of Hadrian, collated and arranged in orderly fashion. This was supplemented in 533 by an edition of the rulings and precedents of classical Roman lawyers called the Digest or Pandects; and in the same year a handbook for law students was published called the Institutes. The whole of this Corpus of Civil Law was written in Latin, the native language of Justinian and still the official language of the Empire. But it is significant that most of the new laws or Novels appended to it were phrased in Greek, the spoken language of the majority of the citizens in the eastern part of the Empire. For this was not simply a lawyers' collection of the imperial ordinances of ancient Rome, harking back to the past. It was an adaptation to meet the needs of a Christian state and society in the present and for the future; and even Justinian had to admit that the Greek language was fast superseding Latin as the general means of communication in the most flourishing portion of his Empire. In one of his Novels he declared: 'We have composed this decree not in the native language but in the spoken tongue of Greek, so that it may be rendered more easily intelligible to all.'

Succeeding emperors such as Leo III and Leo VI produced new legal codes to meet the changing requirements of society. But the Codex of Justinian formed the basis of all law and order in the Byzantine Empire until the fifteenth century. The Slav peoples within and beyond the imperial frontiers in due course adapted it to their own purposes; and its rediscovery by the lawyers of Bologna and the German Emperor Frederick Barbarossa in the twelfth century had profound repercussions on the development of the imperial idea in western Europe. For Justinian's law laid great emphasis on the autocratic power of the Emperor and left little room for doubt about the legal foundation of imperial authority over the Church as well as the State.

Justinian would like to have been remembered as the restorer of the Roman Empire. But his codification of the law was a more lasting memorial than all his military conquests.

The Influence of the Byzantine Church

Deno John Geanakoplos

Although the split between Roman Catholic and Eastern Orthodox, or Byzantine, Christianity did not become official until 1054, the two churches were growing apart by the time that Justinian I became Byzantine emperor in 527. Among other issues, the Byzantines refused to accept the authority of the pope in faraway Rome.

In the following selection, Byzantine historian Deno John Geanakoplos asserts that the Eastern Orthodox Church was the major source of vitality in the Byzantine world. Christianity, he claims, is the combination of Christian thinking with Greek philosophy, which was still very popular and well-known in Byzantine times. In addition, Byzantine religious institutions influenced the later development of the Greek and Russian Orthodox churches, as did Byzantine rituals and practices. Finally, religion helped to give the empire its structure; the rather elaborate Church bureaucracy was repeated in the empire's administration.

Deno John Geanakoplos is professor of history and religious studies at Yale University.

The Byzantine Empire was, technically at least, the Christian form or continuation of the old pagan Roman Empire. By the mid-seventh century, however, it had become almost entirely Greek in culture and outlook; and through the eleventh, and in certain respects up to the thirteenth or even fourteenth centuries, it remained, socially and culturally speaking, the most advanced—certainly the most sophisticated—state in

Excerpted from Deno John Geanakoplos, *Interaction of the "Sibling" Byzantine and Western Cultures in the Middle Ages and Italian Renaissance (330–1600)*. Copyright © 1976 Yale University Press. Reprinted with permission from Yale University Press.

the world. Its gold coin, the *nomisma*, was universally accepted as a kind of dollar of the age. And the refinements of life in Constantinople were legendary not only in the Latin and Arab worlds but even among such semibarbaric peoples as the Vikings of distant Scandinavia. Perhaps one can most readily grasp the importance of the Byzantine state by noting that at the apogee of its power in the early eleventh century, its capital city, Constantinople, contained some eight hundred thousand to one million people, while Paris, perhaps the greatest city of the West, had a mere fifty thousand inhabitants.

There is no need to elaborate further on the preeminence of this state as compared to others of the age, nor to expatiate on the reasons for its decline or its remarkable longevity and tenacity of life, surrounded, as it was, almost continuously by a host of enemies. The significance of the political and economic role of Byzantium is generally recognized today; but its civilization, the accomplishments of its church in particular, are still too little appreciated. Indeed, Byzantine culture is too often regarded not only as something long since dead, but as being of little relevance to the modern Western world. Aside from long-standing Western prejudices arising from the ecclesiastical schism between Rome and Constantinople, a fundamental reason for such neglect is the simple fact that Byzantium as a state no longer exists, though to be sure the modern Greeks, because of a linguistic and religious sense of continuity, believe themselves (and probably rightly) to be the chief legatees of Byzantine civilization.

Byzantine Culture Combined
Christianity and Greek Philosophy

Perhaps a more important reason for the neglect of Byzantium's accomplishments is the all too common view that Byzantine culture, though highly refined, was essentially uncreative and unoriginal. And that factor, rightly or wrongly, is for contemporary critics too often the primary criterion for evaluating the worth of artistic or literary expression. While realizing that without Byzantium virtually all of ancient Greek literature and philosophy would have been lost to the modern world, modern scholars at the same time tend to relegate Byzantium to the role of a mere *passive* repository of ancient culture. This is a one-sided view, for in a number of respects Byzantine civilization may be said to have been highly creative; and this creativity, as will be shown, was in no small measure the result of the synthesis, the intermixture, of the thought and ideas of Hellenistic Greek culture with those of Christianity. It was the transformation effected by the amalgamation of these two forces, and especially the spiritual enrichment afforded by the peculiarly Byzantine brand of Christianity (today called Greek Orthodoxy), that gave Byzantine civilization its unique ethos and vitality.

There is no need to analyze this process of fusion between Greek philosophy and literature on the one hand and Christianity on the other or, as scholars put it more simply, between classical reason and Christian faith. It is pertinent, nevertheless, to cite the judgment of the famous German scholar Werner Jaeger, who declared that "the future of Christianity as a world religion depended on this fusion." In the formative early centuries of the church, the period of the ecumenical councils, the Greek Fathers, who played the leading role, in order better to explain rationally the complexities of Christian dogma, often drew on concepts and terms from ancient Greek philosophy, from Platonism, Stoicism, and Aristotelianism. And in this same early period, although many considered Christianity the enemy and even the negation of pagan Greek culture, the leading Greek Fathers advocated with certain exceptions the study of ancient Greek literature and philosophy. St. Basil himself, the "patron" of Orthodox education, in a famous discourse advised (with qualification) the Christian youth to study ancient Greek literature because its ethical values, so similar in general to those of Christianity, were presented in a style remarkable for its persuasiveness and richness.

Out of the synthesis of these two elements, then—Christianity and Greek thought—a dynamic theology was created. And it was this Greek theology that was primarily responsible for the formulation of Christian philosophy and dogma for the entire Christian church. Though certainly not overlooking the fusion of these two elements, Western scholars sometimes forget that it was the Greek East that developed the so-called apophatic approach to theology, the attempt to explain God by a process of negation—that is, by stating what God is not rather than what he is. For if one tries to define what God *is*, then by implication one tends to limit his nature; and God, of course, is uncircumscribable.

No Separation of Church and State

Another aspect of the Byzantine church and its activities that merits attention is the high degree of lay participation in church affairs. That was, in part, a result of the ideology of Byzantium. For church and state were closely associated, in fact intertwined. They constituted one organic structure, the whole being an imitation (*mimesis*) on earth of the kingdom of heaven above. Over this entire structure on earth presided the Basileus, or emperor, as the representative of God. As a semisacerdotal figure, though technically still a layman, the emperor possessed certain liturgical privileges reserved only for the clergy. He could cross before the Iconostasis and during the liturgy, preach to the congregation and cense the people. He could even communicate himself—that is, administer the bread and wine of the Eucharist to himself. (To be sure, only a priest could actually consecrate the bread and wine.) Yet it is of primary importance to note that, despite these extraordinary privileges, the emperor could not, on his own, pronounce on or alter church dogma: for the formulation of dogma the convocation of an ecumenical council was required. Indeed, the traditional Feast of Orthodoxy, the day on which in 843 the icons were officially restored to the church, is significant precisely because certain emperors of the eighth and early ninth centuries were blocked by the church in their efforts to destroy the holy pictures and prohibit their veneration by the people.

Of special interest to modern society should be the role played in the Byzantine church by the so-called archons, the chief lay citizens in the cities of the empire. It was one of the archons' duties to protect the church in their respective areas, and in later local councils held in Constantinople, such as in the eleventh century, they even played a role in internal ecclesiastical affairs. To the considerable degree of lay participation in affairs of the Byzantine church one might also add the fact of the prominence of lay theologians in Byzantium. Both of these points serve to underscore an important difference between the Greek and Roman churches in the Middle Ages. It is, in fact, only in recent years that the Roman church has been witnessing the emergence of a greater voice for laymen in ecclesiastical affairs. . . .

Another aspect of Byzantine ecclesiastical culture that deserves mention for its creativeness is the character of its spirituality. In Orthodox spirituality perhaps the prime concept is that of *theosis*—that is, the belief that through prayer, dedication, and contemplation (*Hesychia* in Greek) one may, already in this life, achieve a degree of mystical union with God. True, the most famous Byzantine Hesychasts, those of the fourteenth century, were monks withdrawn from the world and living on Mount Athos, and their techniques for achieving a state of contemplation were not always accepted. But their influence was felt widely in Byzantine society and soon spread to Bulgaria, whence, ultimately, they had a great influence on the Muscovite *Startsi* (holy men) who, as is well known, played a considerable role in the turbulent political and social life of sixteenth- and seventeenth-century Russia.

Union with God can, of course, also be achieved through receiving the Eucharist, the partaking of the body and blood of Christ under the appearance of the bread and wine—a sacrament that possesses the same degree of efficacy for laymen, clerics, and monks alike. . . .

The Byzantine Administration Mirrored the Byzantine Church

We come finally to an aspect of Byzantine life and civilization with which the church is again closely associated but which is generally overlooked—the Byzantine administrative system. The Byzantine administrative organization, civil as well as ecclesiastic, with its many titles, ranks, insignia, and protocol, was one of the most carefully structured in history. But, like that of Washington D.C. in our day, it grew eventually so complex as to be at times almost unwieldy.

Nonetheless, from two Byzantine treatises on administration that remain, . . . one can see that the system was not static and that throughout the centuries it underwent evolution in response to the demands of a changing society. . . .

The church, though it had some services and officers in common with the state, in the main possessed its own officials and had its own carefully prepared lists of clerical and lay officials attached to or serving it. According to an edict of the sixth-century emperor Justinian, the Cathedral of Hagia Sophia, or the "Great Church" as it was always called, was to be provided with a huge staff of sixty priests, a hundred deacons, forty deaconesses, ninety subdeacons, a hundred readers, twenty-five chanters, and a hundred custodians. The lavishness of the service must have been remarkably impressive. . . .

Indeed, the church was probably the most fundamental force in the creative vitality of Byzantine culture. The unique blend of Byzantine Christianity, Greek (more accurately "Hellenistic") learning, and certain Eastern elements in the mature Byzantine cultural synthesis, still finds its living expression in the Greek Orthodox church, particularly in the institution of the patriarchate of Constantinople. The patriarchate is, in fact, as striking an example as it is possible to find in the modern world, of the continued viability of the most creative of Byzantine institutions, the Eastern Orthodox church.

Chapter 4

The Franks: Kingdom and Empire in the West

Turning Points

IN WORLD HISTORY

The Strengths and Weaknesses of the Merovingian Kings

Colin Davies

The Franks were one of many Germanic tribes who established independent kingdoms in western Europe after the disappearance of the Roman Empire. Frankish territories were in Roman Gaul, a region which included parts of modern France and Germany. Ultimately, the Franks became the most powerful of the Germanic peoples.

Among the great advantages of the Franks was their early conversion to western Christianity, which gave them the support of the papacy. The ruling dynasty of the king who undertook the conversion, Clovis, was known as the Merovingians, after a legendary leader of the Franks. The Merovingians ruled the Franks from the time of Clovis's death in 511 until 752.

As Colin Davies points out in the following selection, Clovis and his immediate successors were strong warriors, which helped them to establish authority in a violent and unstable era. However, as Davies suggests, certain weaknesses reduced their authority as western Europe became more settled. First, it was Frankish custom for a king to divide his lands among his sons. In Clovis's case, four semi-independent states replaced a unified kingdom, making the entire unit more difficult to govern. Secondly, Merovingian leaders allowed other Frankish nobles, as well as the church, to acquire more land and power, especially in the eighth century. The Arnulfings, or Carolingians, were one of these newly powerful families.

Colin Davies taught history at Repton and St. Paul's Colleges at Cambridge University before going on to become the head of the department of history at Charterhouse School in England.

Excerpted from Colin Davies, *The Emergence of Western Society* (New York: Humanities Press, 1970). Reprinted with permission from Palgrave Publishers Ltd.

The Franks started off with at least three advantages. The events of the fifth and sixth centuries gave their rulers, who were still in essence war-lords, an unparalleled military reputation in the west. Their orthodoxy held out the prospect of a mutually convenient alliance with the church, while the nature and numbers of their settlement in Roman Gaul led first to the peaceful co-existence of Roman and Germanic society, and then to a fusion of the two. Francia was large, fertile, and with enough room for everyone so that there was no incentive to overthrow the existing order. First, the Roman agricultural organisation and techniques were adopted; then the Roman administrative system was followed by both lay and ecclesiastical authorities. On the face of it the fusion of well-tried Roman methods and a new people who were vigorous and willing to learn promised well. As it happened the weaknesses within Frankish society were equally great.

The Warrior Kings of the Franks

Clovis had been a fighter and so were his successors. He had been fortunate in his times; his able generalship could exploit the weaknesses of his neighbours. In this way aggressive instincts were largely directed outwards, extending Frankish power and gaining considerable plunder, always a significant source of revenue for the Frankish kings. By the late sixth century this was no longer the case; the Visigoths were safe behind the Pyrenees, while the Lombards were firmly in control of northern Italy. Further expansion was difficult and this reduced the royal income and fermented endless feuds and civil wars within Francia itself. It was possible to expand directly to the south: in 532 the Burgundian kingdom was overrun and its king, Sigismund, and his family ended up at the bottom of a well. It would be completely misleading to interpret Frankish difficulties in terms of outside pressures: a strong king could always control the restless energies of his subjects. The greatest weakness of the Franks lay in their system of inheritance; the Merovingians regarded their kingdom simply as private property which by Frankish laws was divided up among the heirs. The prospects were gloomy. Assuming the dynasty was fertile, there would either be civil war until the strongest or the most cunning member ousted his rivals, or there would be a passive acceptance of perpetual fragmentation. Either way there would be war and probably a proliferation of petty kingdoms. The Salian system of division had its influence on the later French practice of inheritance; one of the long-term results was the great medieval *apanage*, and the near-independence of states like Burgundy in the fifteenth century. For the later kings of France the system was only dangerous if the monarch was weak in character or resources, or if there was a long-term conflict with another country as in the case of the Hundred Years' War. Under normal circumstances the king could command sufficient loyalty from his vassals and had devised an adequate administration, as well as alliances with the church and the towns, to minimise the danger. With the early Franks this was not so, and the inheritance system threatened anarchy at all times and opened the way to it on numerous occasions from the death of Clovis to the final disintegration of the Carolingian house after 840.

Clovis Divides His Kingdom

In 511 Francia was split between the four sons of Clovis. Theodoric had his capital at Reims, Chlodomir at Orleans, Childebert at Paris, and Chlotar (Lothar) at Soissons. The only motive to inspire co-operation was external danger, and petty dynasties did manage to unite for operations of that sort. Otherwise longevity was the best hope for restoring authority; by 558 Chlotar was the sole survivor but then three years later he died and a new quadripartite division took place. This inaugurated a long period of civil war, marching and countermarching, assassination and political manœuvres of tedious and profitless complexity. The most significant development in the years between the death of Chlotar in 561 and the accession of the last great Merovingian, Dagobert, in 629 was that three large territorial divisions crystallised within the limits of Francia, though their precise boundaries were far from stable. To the north and east, stretching from the Rhine and beyond westwards to the area around Reims, was Austrasia; in the centre was Neustria running from the Channel to the Loire; while in the south Burgundy spread westwards from the Rhone valley to take in large parts of Aquitaine. Neustria at that time carried with it the most prestige and included Paris, but Austrasia was ultimately going to be more important. The latter was more difficult to control, with its dangerously long and exposed frontiers which had no clear geographical terminus beyond the Rhine. The eastern flank was now threatened by the turbulent Saxons, or tribes which were being pushed west by the Slavs and Magyars of central Europe. In 614 Chlotar II had, by accident and design, become sole king of the Franks, and authorised three administrations for Austrasia, Neustria and Burgundy in which the chief official was to be the mayor of the palace. In fact, from the time of Dagobert's death in 639, the history of the Franks revolved round the rival mayors of Neustria and Austrasia rather than the individual kings.

The long civil wars of the later sixth century gave the Frankish rulers ample opportunity to devise imaginative fates for their rivals. The trouble began with the death of Chlotar in 561 when two of his four sons became bitter rivals. Sigebert originally had the lands between the Meuse and the Rhine, while his brother Chilperic (the son of another marriage and considered illegitimate by his brothers) ruled in Soissons and Tournai. The territorial settlement of 561 was politically unwise, but the real trouble came with the marriage of Sigebert to the Visigothic princess Brunhilde. This was a distinguished match, and, not to be outdone, Chilperic married her sister Galswintha. To do this he had put away his mistress, but when he decided to take her up again, the unsatisfactory *ménage* led Galswintha to complain. The result was settlement by subtraction: Galswintha was strangled. This started off a feud led by Brunhilde, whose real ambition was to rule all the Franks. She played off one side against the other for generations, ruling first through her son and then through her grandson until the end came in 613. Having manipulated the succession for some years in Neustria and Austrasia, she was taken prisoner by Chlotar II of Neustria, charged with causing the death of ten kings (the total was not quite so high since Chlotar had been responsible for some of

them), and then tortured for three days. After that she was
tied to the tail of a wild horse and torn to shreds. Contemporary chroniclers made pious comparisons with the fate of
Jezebel who was devoured by hungry dogs.

Chlotar's son Dagobert (629–39), the last distinguished
Merovingian, had been initiated into the arts of government
in Austrasia in 623 under the tutelage of Arnulf, bishop of
Metz, and Pepin I, mayor of the palace. To govern Francia
more effectively he left Austrasia for the more central lands
of Neustria, and established himself at Paris to the chagrin of
his eastern subjects. His influence was felt in the politics of
Italy and Spain, and in the east, despite a setback in 632, he
united the German peoples against the Slavs. The price of
this alliance or federation was the end of the annual tribute of
500 cows from the Saxons, and an independent duke for the
Thuringians. The decisive nature of his leadership brought
the Bavarians over to the Frankish side while his creation of
a neutral zone of loose peripheral alliances prefigured Carolingian policy on this long and insecure frontier.

The Slow Decline of Merovingian Authority

The anonymous chronicler who has been dubbed by historians as Fredegar (Fredegarius Scholasticus) is one of the few
useful sources for these years. Those who continued the
chronicle down to 768 were part of the Arnulfing circle and,
with the wisdom of hindsight reinforced by personal loyalties, their account concentrated on the emergent Arnulfings
or Carolingians who were mayors of the palace in Austrasia.
Fredegar calls the successors of Dagobert 'lesser beasts', and
the long twilight of Merovingian rule and the relations between the kings and their mayors of the palace is the central
and fascinating issue of the period from 639 to 751. The *rois
fainéants* [declining kings] were certainly shadowy figures;
they tended to die young and were physically feeble so that
in the end they were parodied as impotent, parochial figure-
heads who were trundled about their estates in ox-carts.

The original justification for Merovingian kingship had
been ability on the battlefield. This was no longer true. The
most prominent battle of these years was that at Tertry in 687

when the power of the Neustrian mayors of the palace was smashed finally by Pepin II, the mayor of Austrasia. The Arnulfings had taken over as military leaders but they did not take over as kings until 751. The issue involved far more than military leadership. Clovis had been crowned by holy oil sent from heaven, and the close relationship between the church and the monarchy gave an intangible and sacrosanct quality to the anointed Merovingians, however supine they might be as rulers. Longevity is not necessarily a prescription for effective kingship, but it helps if the rulers lack outstanding ability; the later Merovingians had neither the one nor the other. Yet the real key to the problem lies elsewhere: no medieval king could get far without broad acres and a good many of them. Land was the primary source of wealth in any society which had passed beyond plundering without reaching the industrial stage. Kings needed very ample estates to reward loyal followers, endow the church, and yet have enough left to support their own dignities and contribute to the expenses of government. In this respect the crown's own resources had to be very much greater than those of any of the nobility and here the Merovingians were particularly weak. Far too much of the royal fisc [financial power] had been alienated to the church or the nobles; indeed, the key to Merovingian ineffectiveness lay in such poverty, just as the survival of the church and the waxing power of the Arnulfings can be traced to the same cause. By the eighth century the church owned or possessed something like a third of the Frankish lands. Meanwhile the house of Pepin had established itself firmly with estates in the northeast in the Ardennes and in Brabant. Their steady accumulation and sound estate management also meant that the Arnulfings had enough over to endow religious houses such as Nivelles and Andenne and encourage the Hiberno-Roman missions in Utrecht. In yet another field the Arnulfings were able to assume the lead which had once been the distinguishing mark of the reigning dynasty.

From the Merovingians to the Carolingians

R. Allen Brown

Of the various Germanic tribes who dominated western Europe after the fall of Rome, the Franks emerged as the most influential. One reason was their early conversion to Roman Catholic Christianity under King Clovis, who reigned from 482 until 511. From the time of Clovis, the Franks had a close association with the pope, the head of the Roman Catholic Church.

Clovis belonged to a ruling dynasty known as the Merovingians, who led the Franks until the 700s. By that time they had grown weak, and they were threatened by a new, more vigorous Frankish family, the Carolingians. The reputation of the Carolingians was only strengthened by Charles Martel's victory over the Muslims in 732. Yet the Carolingians could not be named Kings of the Franks without the direct approval of the pope.

In the following selection, R. Allen Brown describes how Pepin III, Charles Martel's son, was able to convince the pope that the Carolingians, not the Merovingians, were the true defenders of the Roman church. Moreover, Brown asserts, the status of Germanic kings increased greatly when Pope Stephen II recognized the Carolingians as being kings chosen by God.

R. Allen Brown is professor of medieval history at King's College, London.

Frankia after the death of Clovis [king of the Franks from 482–511] was torn by civil wars, for the kingship, being personal, was divided among the sons or descendants of the

Excerpted from R. Allen Brown, *The Origins of Modern Europe: The Medieval Heritage of Western Civilization.* Copyright © 1972 R. Allen Brown.

dead king like any other Frankish property. Though the later Merovingians produced one great figure in the person of Dagobert (629–639) who happened to succeed to the whole inheritance, anarchy again followed him, with the kingdom threatening to fall apart into the provinces and arbitrary divisions of Austrasia, Neustria and Burgundy, while Aquitaine in the south-west was already in practice independent, and the kings themselves were increasingly ineffective puppets manœuvred by rival noble factions and their power in the hands of their chief official, the Mayor of the Palace (*major domus*).

Charles Martel and the Franks Defeat a Muslim Invasion

In this violent world of high but personal politics, where the stakes were death by assassination or wealth beyond the dreams of avarice, there emerged to pre-eminence the house and family of the Arnulfings, the descendants of St. Arnulf, bishop of Metz (d. 641), as mayors of the palace in Austrasia, one of whom, Pepin of Herstal or Pepin the Young, managed to gather the government of all Neustria and Burgundy as well as Austrasia into his hand. When he died in 714 his son, Charles Martel or Charles the Hammer, albeit illegitimate (by a concubine called Alpais), was able to succeed him as the effective ruler of the kingdom, and he it was who in 732 near Poitiers defeated a Moslem army invading southern Gaul from Spain. And here we pause, for this, with hindsight, is generally regarded as the decisive battle which stopped in the West the hitherto invincible advance of Islam, and the victory was won by Charles Martel, the leader of the Franks and the founder of the Carolingian dynasty which takes its name from him.

But Charles Martel was not yet King of the Franks when he died in 741. That fateful elevation was achieved by his son and successor in the mayoralty, Pepin III, the Short, who, having first obtained the opinion of Pope Zacharias 'that it was better that he who wielded the power should be called king than he who remained without royal power,' was crowned thus with Papal approval and by the hands of St.

Boniface in 751 at Soissons, the last Merovingian king, Childeric III, being deposed and sent to a monastery, the tonsure removing his royal locks. 'Samuel had anointed David king in the place of Saul, and so the Church, aware of the parallel, anointed Pepin and his successors. The Franks were the Chosen of the Lord and their armies the columns of Israel'. Indeed the occasion and the method employed by Pepin to carry out his *coup d'état* of 751 fairly bristle with significance. To depose the Merovingians, however effete, and to deprive them of their blood-right, was a serious matter, and to raise up himself and his house in their stead required some element of legitimacy and divinity to replace that which was broken. That element Pepin obtained from the Church, who, in the person of St. Boniface, not only crowned but anointed him as king in 751, while three years later the new Pope, Stephen II, further anointed and consecrated him king, together with his two sons Charles and Carloman—'Stephen the Pope . . . consecrated him in the honour of the royal dignity by a sacred anointing, and with him his two sons'.

The Carolingian Kings as Protectors of the Church

Though there were then special circumstances and though there will afterwards be further developments, it is on this double occasion of 751 and 754 that the sacring of kings begins, to be carried over also to other nations, and with it the nature of kingship changes from the comparatively irresponsible Germanic lordship of a war-leader wielding a personal regality over his followers to the responsible concept of Christian kingship. King by the Grace of God, anointed with holy oil and consecrated in the sacrament of his coronation as a bishop was consecrated, the monarch will henceforth be part priest as well as king, the defender of the Church and of the Faith, as much responsible for the soul's health of his subjects as for their material well-being and his own. . . .

There are other implications of the events of 751 and 754. . . . By unction and by blessing the Church and the Papacy legitimized the usurpation of the Carolingians, and greatly strengthened—indeed, virtually created—their claim to the kingship thereby. Thus Pope Stephen II in 754, blessing in their turn the sons of Pepin 'with the grace of the Holy Spirit', bound the Franks 'by an interdiction and the threat of excommunication that they should never in future presume to choose a king sprung from the loins of any save those whom the divine piety has deigned to exalt and has purposed to confirm and consecrate'—*i.e.* the Carolingians. So too, more generally, the power and status of kingship were greatly increased by the monarch's new sacerdotal role as a vicar of God on earth, and his authority raised thereby to the level of theocracy. Yet also, to follow another train of thought, a limit has been set to that authority, since the responsibilities of Christian Kingship bring standards to be judged by, and the Christian King must be subject to Divine Law of which the Church is the custodian. Similarly, a third element, that of the Church, has been brought into the making, which involves the selection of kings, hitherto created only by bloodright and that recognition of the most suitable member of the royal kin which is the 'elective' element in early kingship. Finally, if within the kingdom of the Franks Church and State, *regnum* [kingship] and *sacerdotium* [defense of the Church], were henceforth to be brought ever closer to the point of being almost indistinguishable, the events of 751 and 754 have a further significance of great moment as marking the beginning of a lasting alliance between the Papacy and the Franks which will bring about, amongst other things, the Empire of Charlemagne. It was a very real alliance, of this world as well as the next, signalized as when in 755 and again in 756, to carry out his part of the bargain of 751 and 754, King Pepin marched into Italy to defend the Pope against the Lombards, and made over to him the government of what will be the Papal States. And the further significance of these events is that the Papacy, threatened in Italy and despairing of help from Constantinople and the surviving Roman Empire of Byzantium, is perforce turning more and more towards the new, barbarian West, dominated by the Franks but of which it could claim the leadership through the apocryphal 'Donation of Constantine'. Add the close and special relationship of the Papacy with new Christian and Catholic England, add the papally orientated reform of the Frankish Church now put in hand by the Carolingians, and one begins to see the emergence of a Latin Christendom whose distinctive qualities also mean a widening break between East and West.

Charlemagne's Coronation as Holy Roman Emperor

Louis Halphen

The greatest of the Carolingian kings of the Franks was Charles the Great, or Charlemagne, who reigned from 768 to 814. As a military leader he was very successful, adding Italy and parts of Germany to the domains he already controlled in modern-day France and central Europe. In addition, he re-established contact with the Byzantine world to the east. The most memorable event of his reign, however, was his coronation as Holy Roman Emperor on Christmas Day, 800.

In the following selection, Louis Halphen describes how the papacy had grown dependent on the Frankish king for military and political support by the end of the 700s. Charlemagne, Halphen claims, understood this and began to think of himself as the head of western Christendom. It was made official when Pope Leo III placed a crown on his head and referred to him as the new Roman emperor, or "Augustus." What both Charlemagne and Leo III hoped to create was a new, western Christian version of the earlier Roman empire.

Louis Halphen was a renowned historian of medieval Europe in the first half of the twentieth century. He taught for many years at universities in France.

In the course of the events that occurred in Italy since Charlemagne's intervention in Lombard affairs the West had, around him and through him, achieved full consciousness of its unity over against the 'Roman Empire' which, while pursuing its secular career in the Eastern Mediter-

Excerpted from Louis Halphen, *Charlemagne and the Carolingian Empire* (Amsterdam: North-Holland Publishing Company, 1977).

ranean, continued to embody the tradition of ancient Rome. Withdrawn to the 'New Rome' on the Bosporus, this empire preserved no more of its ancient territories west of the Adriatic and Ionian Seas than a few stray pieces whose potential for the future was negligible. The papacy itself had given up looking to the successor of Constantine and Theodosius for protection, and had turned resolutely towards the Carolingians with whom it henceforth felt united through common interests; and with the papacy all of the West, or at least all of the continental West, had at last realized that if it rallied around the conqueror of Saxony, it would gain in strength and opportunities for the future.

The Pope Needs the Support of the King of the Franks

At the very end of the eighth century, after the death of Pope Hadrian I on 25 December 795, this situation became still more evident. Having originally been employed in the ranks of the small clerks in the offices of the Lateran and having risen step by step from the lowliest to the highest posts in the papal palace, to be promoted finally to the Sovereign Pontificate on 26 December 795, Hadrian's successor, Leo III, had felt, more than any other pope, the need to ensure the Frankish king's complete support of his rule. The reservations which Hadrian had still believed himself in a position to make, the resistance he had thought necessary to put up against his colleague's encroachments, were no longer opportune: from the moment of his succession, Leo, accepting facts as they were, treated Charlemagne with the regard due to a ruler and resigned himself to being no more than a docile subordinate beside him. He let pass without protest the letter in which the Frankish king, congratulating him on his elevation to the throne of St Peter, doubtless in [the Chronicles] Alcuin's phrasing, thought fit to remind him that he counted on him to work "for the consolidation of his own patriciate", that is to say, of his rule over Rome as patrician of the Romans, and then added these pregnant sentences:

> I desire to establish with your Beatitude an inviolable pact of faith and charity, through which . . . the apostolic benedic-

tion will be able to follow me everywhere and the most Holy
See of the Roman Church will be constantly protected by my
devotion. It is my duty, with the aid of the Divine Mercy, to
defend the holy Church of Christ by arms everywhere: without, against the incursions of the pagans and the devastations
of the infidels; within, by being her patron in the dissemination of the catholic faith. Your duty, most Holy Father, is to
raise your hands towards God as did Moses and through
your prayers to hasten the success of our arms. . . . Let your
Prudence hold fast to the canonical regulations in all matters
and follow constantly the rules established by the holy fathers so that your life will provide the example of holiness to
all, and let only pious exhortations leave your lips so that
your light may shine before all men.

Thus restricting the pope to prayer, Charlemagne reserved the whole domain of action for himself. The bearer
of the letter, his trusted counsellor Angilbert, had even been
charged to see carefully to the proper distribution of these
tasks. His instructions were:

Be sure to warn the pope that he is expected to live hon-
ourably and above all to observe the sacred canons; tell him
that he should govern the holy Church of God piously according to the agreements you make between you and according to his own conscience. Repeat to him often that the
honour to which he has just acceded is a transitory thing,
whereas the reward for good deeds is eternal. Persuade him
to exert himself with the greatest diligence to root out the
heresy of simony that is defiling the holy body of the Church
in many places. Tell him what you remember about the
problems discussed between us. . . . May the Lord guide and
direct his heart in all goodness, so that he will be able to
serve the holy Church of God effectively and to intercede
with the Almighty in our favour.

This is equivalent to saying that even the spiritual guidance of the Western World was henceforth claimed by the
Frankish king.

Leo III apparently resigned himself more easily to this situation since his personal position was more uncertain. His

election, carried out by surprise the day after Hadrian's death, had encountered in Rome an opposition that, in the summer of 798, had degenerated into riots. The following spring a sensational event occurred. On 25 April 799, as he went in procession from the Lateran to the church of San Lorenzo in Lucina, Leo III was attacked by a group of conspirators. This happened with the complicity of two high officials of the papal palace, one of whom was his predecessor's own nephew. He was thrown on the ground, beaten black and blue, and was subjected to odious and cruel violence; they attempted to tear out his tongue and put out his eyes, and finally they set him on his feet again, covered in blood, only to throw him into a cell of the monastery of St Erasmus, from where only the timely intervention of two *missi* [representatives] of the Frankish king succeeded in rescuing him. But the conspirators had not disbanded and they overwhelmed the pope with their accusations, calling him, among other things, an adulterer and a perjurer. Who, other than Charles himself, was capable of delivering the papacy from this impasse? In the heart of Saxony, where he was still grappling with the pagans, the pope's desperate appeal reached him. . . .

Charlemagne as the Head of All Western Christians

Meanwhile during the summer of 799 everything combined to strengthen Charlemagne's position and to cause the notion to prevail that he was the supreme arbiter of the West. The arrival of the pope who, having scarcely recovered from his wounds, had come to the heart of Saxony to ask Charlemagne for help, had made a great impression. In an epic composition, written shortly after the encounter, a poet believed to be Angilbert took it as his text to glorify, in sonorous verse and with many hyperbolic epithets, "the king Charles, head of the world and pinnacle of Europe" alone capable of "subjecting [the pope's] conduct to a fair judgment" and to "avenge the cruel blows" that he had been dealt. Among the flood of classical allusions in his writings, the poet twice uses, in reference to Charlemagne, the epithet 'august'. Three times he even calls him "the Augustus", "the great Augustus",

Charles, who became king of the Franks and Holy Roman Emperor Charle-magne (right) is notified of the death of his father King Pepin.

implying by this that in his eyes the Frankish king actually occupied in the Europe of that time—and the name 'Europe' was familiar to him—the position of an Augustus.

In the same period and under the impression of the same events Theodulf, the bishop of Orleans, addressed a complimentary poem to the king in which, after having recalled that Charlemagne was "the honour and the glory of the Christian people", he did not scruple to write that it was St Peter himself who, "desiring to find a substitute for himself in him", "had sent him to rescue" the pope. "He who has the keys of heaven" he continues, "has ordained that you will have them" and he concludes: "You rule the Church . . . the clergy and the people."

Finally, at the moment when Charles, after having in the autumn of 799 caused Leo III to be escorted back into his capital, made himself ready to join him there to investigate on the spot the guilt incurred by the conspirators as well as by the pope himself, Alcuin, completely opposed as he had from the first been to any kind of procedure against the Sovereign Pontiff, could not refrain from addressing to his "precious David"—that was the Frankish king's nickname—a small poem in which his hopes and wishes are expressed in elegant verse. Might he dress the wounds from which Rome suffered, re-establish harmony between the pope and the people, restore order and bring well-being to all. "Rome, capital of the world, sees in you its protector", he writes; cause "peace and piety" to reign there anew; "guide the ruler of the Church, the Lord guiding you yourself with His mighty hand". A conclusion which, as we can see, agrees with that of Theodulf; Charlemagne, placed at the top of the earthly hierarchy, becomes the immediate deputy of God for all the Christians of the West including the Sovereign Pontiff himself.

The King of the Franks
Becomes Holy Roman Emperor

It was certainly with this in mind that Charlemagne started on his way to Rome in the autumn of 800; and his journey turned into a triumph. The pope, not yet cleared of the grave accusations with which the Romans continued to attack him, came to meet Charlemagne at Mentana, twenty kilometres from the city, whence he returned hastily to prepare a reception worthy of his illustrious visitor. The following day, 24 November 800, he received the Frankish king with great pomp, at the top of the steps of St Peter's, surrounded by all his clergy and amidst a chorus of thanksgiving. . . .

On 25 December, when Charles had returned to St Peter's for the feast of Christmas and had kneeled, prior to the celebration of divine service, to pray before the 'confession' of the Prince of the Apostles, Pope Leo approached him, and at the moment Charlemagne rose placed on his head a crown while the 'Roman people' thrice shouted the

Charlemagne's Plans for His Children

According to Einhard, the chronicler of the life of Charlemagne, the King of the Franks and Holy Roman Emperor hoped to train his children both according to the liberal arts and more practical skills: warfare and horsemanship for the boys, spinning and weaving for the girls.

The plan that he adopted for his children's education was, first of all, to have both boys and girls instructed in the liberal arts, to which he also turned his own attention. As soon as their years admitted, in accordance with the custom of the Franks, the boys had to learn horsemanship, and to practise war and the chase, and the girls to familiarize themselves with cloth-making, and to handle distaff and spindle, that they might not grow indolent through idleness, and he fostered in them every virtuous sentiment.

Selection from Einhard, *Life of Charlemagne*, translated by E.E. Turner, reprinted in *The Eagle, the Crescent, and the Cross: Sources of Medieval History*, Volume I. New York: Appleton-Century-Crofts, 1967.

acclamation: "To Charles Augustus, crowned by God, great and pacific emperor of the Romans, life and victory!" After which the Pontiff, prostrating himself before the new Augustus "adored him", as the ancient imperial protocollary formula inaugurated under Diocletian has it. Thus, by a sensational turn of events, quietly prepared during the preceding weeks and perhaps months, Charles suddenly found himself raised to the dignity of Roman emperor.

The principal object of this ceremonial, copied as it was from the one enacted since the fifth century by the patriarch of Constantinople at the coronation of the Byzantine emperor, was without any doubt the clarification of the existing situation. The title 'patrician of the Romans' was up to then the only one that Charlemagne had made use of in his relations with the Sovereign Pontiff and with the Romans themselves; but none of the prerogatives he had gradually arrogated to himself under cover of this title, which had originally been purely honorary, were legally justified. When, for example, he required from the new popes immediate notification of their election, he usurped a prerogative which, up to the middle of the eighth century, the 'Roman emperors' of Byzantium had continuously exercised. But since then, the situation had imperceptibly changed, so that by Christmas of the year 800 the Frankish king had, with regard to the papacy, already appropriated almost all the prerogatives formerly acknowledged to belong to the emperor. The disputes that had arisen in the relations between the two powers during Hadrian's pontificate had in any case made the inconvenience of a state of affairs so legally ill-defined quite evident. To replace the ambiguous title of 'patrician of the Romans' by the decisive and clear 'emperor of the Romans' was the primary object of the ceremony in St Peter's on 25 December 800, and this was what impressed its contemporaries. The author of the *Royal Annals*, after telling the story of the coronation in almost the same terms as those we have used ourselves, restricts himself to the laconic conclusion ". . . and, discarding his title of patrician, he was called emperor and Augustus.". . .

Once recognized as emperor, Charlemagne exercised power at Rome with a freer hand, and henceforth it was possible to invoke definite precedents to support this. In principle, all ambiguity had now disappeared: traditionally, the emperor was the sovereign of Rome; he spoke there as its lord, judged there as its lord. As regards the pope, he enjoyed the prestige there and the authority attached to the See of St Peter, but was obliged in the exercise of his authority to conform to the rules that for centuries had regulated relations between the two powers: not only should he notify the emperor of his election, but custom decreed that his consecration should be subject to the emperor's consent, and this rule was explicitly recalled at the death of Leo III in 816.

The Carolingian Renaissance in Literacy and Culture

C.W. Previté-Orton

In the following selection, C.W. Previté-Orton claims that the most important legacy of Charlemagne and the Carolingian kings was the cultural rebirth they helped to inspire. This renaissance was to help create a new, western European culture.

In search of ways to train new clergymen, Charlemagne turned his court at Aachen in present-day Germany into a center of learning and scholarship. He attracted scholars, most of whom were monks. These scholars brought with them copies of old manuscripts, and they rediscovered others. In addition, architects and artists became active in trying to revive earlier traditions of church and monument building.

The products of the Carolingian Renaissance, Previté-Orton asserts, were a hybrid of Roman influences, Byzantine traditions, and the more energetic yet barbaric world of the Germans.

C.W. Previté-Orton was professor of medieval history at St. Johns College, Cambridge University.

Not in its ephemeral political structure, but in the realm of thought did Charlemagne's Empire produce durable effects. Its unity was soon broken, its institutions were changed beyond recognition, its prosperity was ruined. Politically Western Europe had almost to start again. Only in the organization of the Church, which was renewed under its shadow, was there an abiding, if maimed, inheritance. But its conception of kingship remained to be an inspiration for the

Excerpted from C.W. Previté-Orton, *The Shorter Cambridge Medieval History Volume I: The Later Roman Empire to the Twelfth Century* (Cambridge: Cambridge University Press, 1966). Reprinted with permission from Cambridge University Press.

future, and its revival of learning and culture and its recovered touch with the remnants of ancient civilization, although much narrower than Charlemagne dreamed and intended, survived the dangers of the next two centuries and formed a foundation for the advance of the Middle Ages. It was the salvage of learning and ancient literature, sprinkled on the verges of the Empire, and now in the 'Carolingian Renaissance' spread over the monasteries and cathedral churches of Francia, that by its extension saved them for transmission to later times.

Between Boethius, 'the last of the Romans' according to a famous phrase, and the height of the Carolingian Renaissance three centuries had intervened. We have seen how Cassiodorus linked the study of Christian and also secular learning with monasticism, and how much of this was brought to English monasteries by Hadrian, Benedict Biscop, and their followers in the seventh century. The movement culminated in the persons of the Venerable Bede and St Aldhelm, perhaps the most learned men of their day in the West, but it continued with less creative vigour in the cathedral school of York, not to mention lesser centres, and its offshoots were already growing in eastern Francia in the monasteries of St Boniface and his fellows. England, however, was by no means the only refuge of literate culture. Manuscripts and some grammatical proficiency survived in Lombard Italy and the Papal Curia. In Visigothic Spain, reinforced by fugitives from Vandal Africa, there existed a living, if decadent, Christian learning and literature, of which St Isidore of Seville was the great exemplar. Further, there was a remarkable focus of ancient learning outside the Roman Empire in Celtic Ireland. There seems to have been an emigration thither of some scholars with books from Aquitaine even before St Patrick's mission. As Ireland became Christian, a knowledge of Latin and even a little Greek was acquired by Irish monks. St Columbanus was a real scholar. Indeed, there are Latin classics which have only survived through the medium at one time of Irish manuscripts. The emigration of Irish monks to the Continent brought Irish learning with it.

Charlemagne's Revival of Education and Literature

It was from these scattered centres of culture that Charlemagne began to develop a real system of education, an attempt to revive the past. His first desire was to obtain an educated clergy to maintain the Faith and the Church, but he himself possessed an eager thirst for knowledge, a vivid interest in literature and the things of the mind. The palace school, where his sons, young nobles, and others were brought up became a home of literary education for such as were apt. The educated layman, though a rarity, made his appearance. Cathedral and monastic schools arose; there was even an attempt to make parish priests undertake teaching. Books were multiplied and monastic libraries enlarged. From Corbie, St Martin of Tours and other abbeys, the clear and beautiful bookhand, the Caroline minuscule, spread and replaced towards the close of the eighth century the decadent, ill-formed, divergent scripts which were current in the several lands of the West. Although some centuries later the Caroline minuscule gave way to pointed fashions of writing, it had imprinted a general unity on bookhands, which played its part in maintaining a unity of culture.

The best of Charlemagne's literary teachers, whom he made his friends, came from outside Francia. The central figure was the Northumbrian Alcuin bred in the school of York, who came at Charlemagne's invitation, and was rewarded with the abbacy of St Martin of Tours. Although quite unoriginal, his wide reading and his accurate scholarship enabled him to be an excellent teacher with many disciples. His writings were voluminous, both verse, letters, school manuals, and theological treatises. In his last years he was busied in preparing a more correct text of the Vulgate Bible, which called a temporary halt to scribal corruption. In this revision he had a less effective rival in the Visigoth Theodulf, Bishop of Orleans, who was the best writer of Latin verse of the day. The best prose writer was the East Frank Einhard from the Maingau: his *Vita Karoli*, succinct, clear, and picturesque, closely modelled in structure and wording on Suetonius, is a worthy monument of his master.

Less classic and more spontaneous was the Lombard grammarian, Paul the Deacon from Friuli, who wrote a graphic history of his own people. The list of these men and their disciples might easily be extended, but in so short a summary it is enough to indicate their work. They restored grammatical Latin and established it in too many cathedral schools and abbeys for it to come to wreck completely again.

Scholars Revive Ancient Classics

As might be expected of men with so much to learn and teach, the work of the Carolingians was rather in the acquisition and divulgation of ancient knowledge and literature than in any original contributions to thought. Only John Eriugena the Scot was an original thinker. But they increased both the copies and the understanding of the Christian Fathers and of the remnant of heathen classics: the oldest manuscripts of most of these date from the Carolingian age. The spate of Carolingian Latin verse was imitative to a degree. In thought, compendiums of excerpts from the Fathers, in which Bede had set an example, were their forte. Hrabanus Maurus (*ob.* 856), Abbot of Fulda and later Archbishop of Mainz, was the most assiduous and learned of this kind of commentator. The Canon Law of the Church found its students and its reforming forgers. Even doctrine had its controversialists. The Adoptionists of Spain, who held that Christ only became the Son of God at His baptism, were countered by the orthodox Alcuin, and the *Libri Carolini* dealt with the iconoclastic dispute. Paschasius Radbert (*ob. c.* 860) upheld the doctrine of Transubstantiation in the Eucharist against Ratramn. The unhappy Gottschalk (*ob.* 869), a compulsory monk and something of a poet, suffered harsh persecution from the dominating Hincmar, Archbishop of Rheims, on account of his rigid view of predestination. This unoriginal age could at least debate old problems.

Historical writing of a sort was practised in certain abbeys. Dry and scrappy chronicles were jotted down—one by Charlemagne's grandson Nithard soars a little higher. The official papal biographies in the *Liber Pontificalis* give facts. But the vivacious *Gesta Karoli*, a repertoire of legends, are more alive, if fabulous: the author was Notker the Stammerer (*ob.* 912) of St Gall, who by his sequences influenced the growth and prosody of religious hymns, and through them of secular verse.

Writings Were in Latin Rather than Local Languages

It is unfortunate that vernacular compositions of native subject-matter in the Frankish Empire before and during the Carolingian age are lacking. Charlemagne's collection of old Frankish lays was destroyed by his son. Only a fragment or so, like that of *Hildebrand*, remain of the old German poems, although Christian lays in native style, like the Saxon *Heliand* (*c.* 830), appeared, and the *Ludwigslied* celebrates a West Frankish victory of 881. The first specimen of Old French, consciously different from Latin, is the oath which Lewis the German took at Strasbourg to be understood of his brother Charles the Bald's West Frankish subjects. For the popular world of the age unhampered by a learned language and redolent of the new peoples, we must mainly go outside the Western Empire. England takes the most conspicuous place. The native codes and chronicles were there written in the native speech. The lay of *Beowulf* (*c.* 700?) preserves Teutonic traditions, only slightly Christianized. A small corpus of Christian poems keep the ancient outlook and technique. The translations made or inspired by King Alfred (*ob.* 899) from Gregory, Orosius, Bede, and Boethius are infused with something of his own great spirit. They were not intended to make his people erudite, but to equip them for a better practical life. The sermons of Aelfric (*ob. post* 1006) show the same purpose with an unaffected ease of style. A highly artificial technique and an unfettered imagination, on the contrary, mark the Irish poems and tales of this early period. The few early Welsh survivals have much the same quality. A more rugged artificiality appears to mark the earliest Scandinavian verse. A merit which they all have in common is to bring us vividly nearer to a barbaric but very human world than the laborious productions of learned, upward-striving cliques.

The history of the arts must be touched on, rather than traced, even more sketchily than that of literature. In Western Europe there were three main influences at work, the Romano-Christian tradition, the inborn native stock, and the steady pressure of Eastern ideas percolating westward by trade, travel, and territorial contact. To these we may add the needs to be satisfied in building, adornment, and instruction. First may be taken the influence of the East, in the main of the Byzantine Empire. It was not only an export from far away, but an existing model in the recently Byzantine lands in Italy.

Byzantine art was the creation of a long-descended and composite civilization still in full career. If it reached its apogee under Justinian, it continued to develop with fertile beauty and originality, while faithful to its dominant ideas. In the churches, the gathering-place of worship, the sacred drama, the gorgeous ritual procession, the chanting choirs, the atmosphere of supernatural awe were given their ideal setting, which demanded and enhanced them. Without pretence and without bungling the builders did what was required in a free and great way in noble materials and under the guidance of a fine tradition. Their principal means were the dome, many-coloured marbles, and mosaic decoration, whether the church were round, quadrangular, or cruciform in its main design. As in the masterpiece of St Sophia, designed by the architects Anthemius and Isidorus from Asia Minor, the outside was plain, if imposing. Within, St Sophia glistened with the many-coloured columns and their carved capitals and the walls and dome encrusted with marble and mosaics, which set off one another with a harmony of contrast. All that could express the glory and the mystery of the cult was there on a magnificent scale. But lesser churches rivalled St Sophia in beauty of design and colour. The mosaics not only contained pictorial teaching with a solemn majesty but their golden backgrounds suffused the churches with a glowing atmosphere. This architecture could be seen in the West at Ravenna and Rome, to mention no other towns, while carved ivories and jewels journeyed westward along with illuminated manuscripts which furnished models for religious iconography.

A Roman and Germanic Synthesis

The Roman-Christian tradition, however, was alive in the West apart from Byzantine novelties. Churches, monuments, and ruins of Roman provincial art (and the metropolitan art of Rome itself) were still extant in Gaul and Italy to give inspiration and guidance to the unpractised hands of barbarized generations. And those new peoples had something to give of their own. There was a barbaric element in their blood and traditions. The Anglo-Saxon school of art which arose in Christian Northumbria in the seventh century shows this blending to perfection. Arts and motives were brought from Italy by such men as Wilfrid and Benedict Biscop. Churches, if small, were built and decorated. Stone crosses were set up with sculptures, which were half-barbaric in their carving, yet so impressive in design that they have been claimed for a later century. The graceful illuminations and the calligraphy of the *Lindisfarne Gospels* (*c.* 700) testify to an exquisite feeling for colour and line. A similar artistic impulse is shown in Irish crosses and still more in the intricate decoration of the *Book of Kells* (*c.* 700) and the beautiful Irish script.

Much in the art of the Carolingian revival was directly derived from the Roman monuments, and men naturally made no distinction between provincial Roman of the West and Byzantine. The great fact was that barbarism took up the arts of civilization. Charlemagne and his court intended to renew ancient Rome. Romanesque art in his Empire is intentional in its use of Roman models. His round palace church at Aachen imitated churches like Justinian's San Vitale at Ravenna and was enriched with columns from Theodoric's palace. Its mosaics were of Italo-Byzantine inspiration. Decorative arts, like those of ivories and enamels, were developed by the impact of the East on the Teutonic craftsman. Superb illuminated gospels, like the *Golden Gospels* of Charlemagne, mingled influences from England and the south. The Frankish Rhineland became a focus of artistic influences. As in learning and literature, the Carolingian Renaissance was the parent of a growing art. Inexpertness and half-barbaric genius allowed the native impulses to break through the crust of borrowed models. Uncouth and stolid figures expressed a fierce and imaginative power. The artists betrayed themselves in attempting what they could not do, in grasping after conceptions which eluded their reach.

Chapter 5

The Early Middle Ages Give Way to the High Middle Ages

Turning|Points

IN WORLD HISTORY

The Muslim Challenge

Henri Pirenne

From the seventh century until well after the year 1000 A.D. the Christian world, both east and west, was beset by a new challenge. A new monotheistic religion, related to both Judaism and Christianity, emerged out of Arabia. The new religion was Islam, and inspired by the faith taught by the prophet Muhammad, Arab warriors soon set up an empire that stretched from Spain in the west to the Byzantine world in the east.

In the following selection, medieval historian Henri Pirenne asserts that the Islamic conquests completely re-configured the Mediterranean world. While the Arab empire provided for trade and cultural contact with Asia, it isolated the Byzantine Empire from western Christendom. After a largely Germanic army, led by Charles Martel of the Franks, prevented a further Islamic conquest of the west at the Battle of Poitiers in 732, western Europe began to go its own way. The new Europe was to be a combination of Germanic traditions and Roman Catholic Christianity.

Henri Pirenne is a leading historian of medieval Europe. He was professor of history at the University of Ghent in Belgium.

In the whole history of the world there has been nothing comparable, in the universal and immediate nature of its consequences, with the expansion of Islam in the 7th century.

The overwhelming rapidity of its propagation was no less surprising than the immensity of its conquests. It took only seventy years from the death of Mohammed (632) to spread from the Indian Ocean to the Atlantic. Nothing could stand

Excerpted from Henri Pirenne, *A History of Europe Volume I: From the End of the Roman World in the West to the Beginnings of the Western States.* Copyright © 1956 University Books, Inc.

before it. At the first blow it overthrew the Persian Empire (637–644); then it deprived the Byzantine Empire, one by one, of each of the provinces which it attacked: Syria (634–636), Egypt (640–642), Africa (698), and Spain (711). The Visigoths had retaken Spain from the Byzantines, and their last king, Roderick, fell in the battle of Cadiz (711).

The onward march of the invaders was checked only at the beginning of the 8th century, when the great movement by which they were threatening Europe from both sides at once was halted beneath the walls of Constantinople (717) and by the soldiers of Charles Martel on the plain of Poitiers (732). It was checked; its first expansive energy was exhausted; but it had sufficed to change the face of the globe. Wherever it had passed the ancient States, which were deeply rooted in the centuries, were overturned as by a cyclone; the traditional order of history was overthrown. This was the end of the old Persian Empire, the heir of Assyria and Babylon; of the Hellenized regions of Asia which had constituted the Empire of Alexander the Great, and had thereafter continued to gravitate in the orbit of Europe; of the ancient Egypt, whose past was still living beneath the Greek veneer that had covered it since the days of the Ptolemies; and of the African provinces which Rome had won from Carthage. Henceforth all these regions were subject, in religion and political obedience, to the most powerful potentate who had ever existed, the Caliph of Baghdad.

Muslim Determination and Arab Conquest

And all this was the work of a nomadic people which had hitherto lived almost unknown in its rock-strewn deserts, which were disdained by all the conquerors, and numbered infinitely fewer inhabitants than Germany. But this people had just been converted by a prophet who had issued from its womb. It had shattered all its old idols, and had suddenly adopted the purest monotheism, and its conception of its duty to God had a formidable simplicity: it was, to obey Allah and compel the infidels to obey Him. The Holy War became a moral obligation, and its own reward. Warriors who fell with their weapons in their hands enjoyed the beatitudes of Paradise. For the rest, the booty of the rich traders who surrounded poverty-stricken Arabia on every side would be the lawful prize of the military apostolate.

There can be no doubt that it was fanaticism—or if you will, religious enthusiasm—that launched the Muslims on the world. Between the invasions of these sectaries, who surged onward invoking Allah, and those of the Germans, who left their country only to acquire more fertile soil, the moral difference is impressive. Yet the social constitution of the Arabs fitted them admirably for their rôle. Nomads and poor, they were fully prepared to obey the command of God. They had only to saddle their horses and set off. They were not, as the Germans were, emigrants dragging behind them women and children, slaves and cattle; they were horsemen, accustomed from childhood to cattle-raids, and now Allah had laid upon them the duty of raiding the world in His name.

It must be admitted, however, that the weakness of their adversaries very greatly facilitated their task. Neither the Byzantine nor the Persian Empire, surprised by the unexpectedness of the attack, was in a condition to resist it. After Justin II the government of Constantinople had grown continually weaker, and nowhere, from Syria to Spain, did the invaders find armies before them. Their fiery onset encountered only disorder. Of the conquests of Justinian nothing was left, after 698, but Italy. Christianity, which had reigned on all the shores of the Mediterranean, now held only the northern shore. Three-fourths of the littoral of this sea, hitherto the common centre of European civilization, now belonged to Islam.

And they belonged to it not only by occupation, but also by virtue of religious and political absorption. The Arabs did not, like the Germans, respect the *status quo* in the conquered territories. They could not. While the Germans, on abandoning their religion for Christianity, immediately fraternized with the Romans, the Muslims appeared as the propagandists of a new faith, an exclusive and intolerant faith to which all had to submit. Religion, wherever they ruled, was the basis of political society; or rather, the religious organization and the political organization were for them identical;

Church and State forming a single unity. The infidels could continue the practice of their cult only as simple subjects, deprived of all rights whatsoever. Everything was transformed, from top to bottom, in accordance with the principles of the Koran. Of the entire administration—justice, finance, the army—nothing was left. Kadis and emirs replaced the exarchs of the country. The Muslim law replaced the Roman law, and the Greek and Latin languages, before which the old national idioms of the coasts of Syria, Africa and Spain had long ago disappeared, were ousted in their turn by the Arabic tongue.

These two elements—religion and language—constitute the Arab's contribution to the Muslim civilization. This civilization, despite its brilliant achievements during the first few centuries of Islam, can boast of little that is original. The conquered peoples were all more refined than their nomad conquerors, and the latter borrowed from them in a wholesale fashion. The Arabs translated the works of their scholars and philosophers, drew inspiration from their art, and adopted their agricultural, commercial and industrial methods. The extent and diversity of the countries and the nations upon which they imposed their rule subjected them to a quantity of influences, which blended together, giving the Muslim civilization an aspect of great variety, but little depth. Of these influences, that of Hellenism rivalled that of Persia. This should not surprise us, when we reflect that the Arabs occupied the richest and most populous sections of the contemporary Greek world—Egypt and Syria.

Their architecture gives us a fairly precise idea of the variety and the relative importance of their borrowings. We see in its decoration characteristics which are evidently of Persian or Indian origin, but the general conception, and the essential members of the buildings, reveal an obvious relationship with Byzantine architecture. The predominance of Greek thought is even more plainly evident. Aristotle was the master of the Arab philosophers, who added nothing essential to his philosophy. On the whole, in the intellectual domain, the Muslim civilization did not greatly influence the European peoples. The explanation is simple: there was much in it that was artificial, and the sources upon which it drew most freely were, for the most part, European sources.

New Connections with Asia

But the case is different in respect of the economic domain. Here, thanks to their contact with the West and the far East, the Arabs were valuable intermediaries. From India they imported sugar-cane into Sicily and Africa, rice into Sicily and Spain (whence the Spaniards took it to Italy in the 15th and 16th centuries), and cotton into Sicily and Africa; they acclimatized in Asia the manufacture of silk, which they learned from the Chinese; and from the Chinese also they learned the use and manufacture of paper, without which the invention of printing would have been valueless, or would not have been made; and from China they imported the magnetic compass. But it was a long while before these innovations— with many more—became the property of the European peoples. At first they only helped to make Islam a more formidable enemy to its European neighbours, as being both richer and more perfectly equipped. From the 7th to the 11th century Islam was incontestably the master of the Mediterranean. The ports which the Arabs constructed—Cairo, which succeeded to Alexandria, Tunis, and Kairouan—were the *étapes* [stages] of a commerce which circulated from the Straits of Gibraltar to the Indian Ocean, through the Egyptian ports, which were in communication with the Red Sea, and the Syrian ports, which gave access to the caravan route to Baghdad and the Persian Gulf. The navigation of the Christian peoples was restricted to a timid coastwise trade along the shores of the Adriatic and southern Italy, and among the islands of the Archipelago.

Muslims Dominate the Mediterranean

An unforeseen event is always followed by a catastrophe in proportion to its importance. It flings itself, so to speak, across the current of historic life, interrupting the series of causes and effects of which this current is constituted, damming them up in some sort, and by their unexpected repercussions overturning the natural order of things. This was what happened at the time of the Muslim invasion. For centuries Europe had gravitated about the Mediterranean. It was by means of the Mediterranean that civilization had extended itself; by means of the Mediterranean the various parts of the civilized world had communicated one with another. On all its shores social life was the same in its fundamental characteristics; religion was the same; manners and customs and ideas were the same, or very nearly so. The Germanic invasion had not changed the situation in any essential respect. In spite of all that had happened, we may say that in the middle of the 7th century Europe still constituted, as in the time of the Roman Empire, a Mediterranean unity.

Now, under the sudden impact of Islam, this unity was abruptly shattered. The greater portion of this familiar sea—which the Romans had called "our sea," *mare nostrum*—became alien and hostile. The intercourse between the West and the East, which had hitherto been carried on by means of this sea, was interrupted. The East and the West were suddenly separated. The community in which they had lived so long was destroyed for centuries to come, and even to-day Europe is still suffering from the consequences of its destruction.

Obliged to meet the menace from the East, the Empire could no longer stand firm on the Danube. The Bulgars, Serbs and Croats spread through the Balkans, and only the cities remained Greek. The invaders did not mingle with the population, as the Germans had done. The Byzantine Empire ceased to be universal; it became a Greek State.

The Bulgars, in 677, subdued the Slav tribes, and became merged with them in Mesia. In the middle of the 9th century their prince, Boris, was converted by Methodius and took the name of Michael.

Western Europe Is Separated from Byzantium

The Byzantine Empire, henceforth confined between the coast of Illyria and the Upper Euphrates, devoted the bulk of its forces to withstanding the pressure of Islam. In its long history, down to the day when it finally succumbed, in the middle of the 15th century, under the blows of the Turks, it was still to know some moments of splendour, and was to witness the development of a civilization whose originality consisted in the blending of ancient traditions with orthodox Christianity and an increasing Orientalization. But this history, most of the time, was alien to that of Western Europe. Venice alone kept in touch with Byzantium, and found, in her rôle of intermediary between East and West, the beginning of her future greatness. For the rest, although Byzantium had ceased to intervene in the West, she none the less continued to exercise an influence which was to outlive her by many centuries. It was Byzantium that Christianized the Slavs of the South and East—the Serbs, Bulgars and Russians—and it was the people of the Empire who, after bearing the Turkish yoke for 400 years, reconstituted the Greek nationality in the 20th century.

As for the West, its separation from Byzantium confronted it with a completely novel situation. This separation seemed to exclude it from civilization, since from the beginning of the ages all the forms of civilized life and all social progress had come to it from the East. True, with the Arabs established in Spain and on the coast of Africa the East was at its door. But in spite of material contact, the difference of religious faith prevented any moral contact between its Christian population and this Muslim Orient. For the first time since the formation of the Roman Empire, Western Europe was isolated from the rest of the world. The Mediterranean by which it had hitherto kept in touch with civilization was closed to it. This, perhaps, was the most important result, as regards the history of the world, of the expansion of Islam. For the Christianity of the West, when its traditional lines of communication were cut, became a world apart, able to count only on itself, and in respect of its further development it was thrown upon its own resources. Driven off the Mediterranean, it turned to the still barbarous regions beyond the Rhine and the shores of the North Sea. European society, continuously expanding, crossed the ancient frontiers of the Roman Empire. A new Europe was created with the rise of the Frankish Empire, in which was elaborated the Western civilization which was one day to become that of the whole world.

The End of the Viking Age

Michael Gibson

The following piece, taken from Michael Gibson's book *The Vikings*, traces the events that led to the end of the Viking era during the middle of the eleventh century. In Gibson's view, social and political changes—both in the Scandinavian world and in Europe at large—reduced the incentives for Vikings to go on raids. For example, he writes, the Western European countries that had once been easy prey for the Vikings had grown stronger and began to fiercely resist the Scandinavian invaders. The spread of Christianity throughout the Viking lands also contributed to the end of the raiders' lifestyle, he maintains. Gibson is the author of numerous histories and biographies, an editor, and an amateur archeologist.

By about 1066, the great days of the Vikings were over. The raids continued for some time, but were increasingly ineffective. What had happened?

Changes in the Viking World

Important social changes had taken place in the Scandinavian communities. In early Viking times there had been many petty kings whose power was confined to their immediate estates. But as the years passed, effective kingdoms were created by strong men like Olaf Tryggvason and Swein Forkbeard. The chieftains, who had played one king off against another, and gone raiding whenever they chose, found themselves reduced to the status of the king's representatives.

The struggle between the kings and the chieftains usually coincided with the battle between paganism and Christianity. Denmark was the first Scandinavian kingdom to be converted.

Excerpted from Michael Gibson, *The Vikings.* Copyright © 1972 Wayland Publishers Ltd. Reprinted with permission from Hodder and Stoughton Publishers.

Harald Bluetooth (945–985) was convinced of the power of Jesus by a brave little priest called Poppo who, according to *Olaf Tryggvason's Saga*, "picked up red hot iron bars and showed his unscorched hands to the King. Thereafter, King Harald and the whole Danish army were baptised."

King Hakon (945–960) was the first Christian King of Norway. But he had to tread carefully: "He was a good Christian when he came to Norway," says *Hakon the Good's Saga*, "but all the land was heathen and as he needed the help and friendship of the people, he decided to conceal his Christianity. When he had established himself in the land and fully subjected it to himself, he sent to England for a bishop and other priests." Norway's conversion was completed by Olaf Tryggvason (995–1000) and St. Olaf (1014–30) who used terrorist methods.

The Swedes clung tenaciously to the old faith. An Anglo-Danish monk wrote gloomily at the beginning of the twelfth century: "As long as things go well, Svear and Goter seem willing to honour Christianity, but when they go wrong and there are bad harvests, droughts, storms, enemy attacks or outbreaks of fire, they persecute the Church they nominally support, not only with words but in deeds. They revenge themselves upon the Christians and seek to chase them right out of the country." Gradually, the Christian priests won and the old religion disappeared. Scandinavia was divided up into bishoprics and parishes and the bishops and priests supported the kings who were their protectors and kept law and order.

The great overseas migration of the Vikings was over. There was nowhere left to colonize—the Western Islands, Iceland and Greenland were fully settled. However, Scandinavian farming methods had improved and more land was brought under cultivation. At last they were able to satisfy their own needs.

Meanwhile, the Norse colonists in Ireland, the English Danelaw, Normandy and Russia were being absorbed by the native populations. They married the local girls and accepted the religion, language and customs of their adopted countries.

Raiding became more difficult: the rulers of Western Europe were stronger in the eleventh century than they had been in the ninth. Everywhere, Viking armies were being bloodily defeated. One of the most celebrated of these defeats took place at Clontarf in Ireland at the hands of the aged Brian Boru in 1014. The following description of the battle is from the medieval text *The War of the Gaedil with the Gaill:* "On one side of the battle were the shouting, hard hearted, murderous Vikings. They had sharp, poisoned arrows which had been dipped in the blood of dragons, toads,

---

A Foreign Impression of Swedish Vikings

In this account from an Arab merchant, the Swedish Vikings who traveled through Russia to the Byzantine Empire appear savage next to the more settled and civilized peoples of the Byzantine world.

I saw the Rus folk when they arrived on their trading-mission and settled at the river Atul (Volga). Never had I seen people of more perfect physique. They are tall as date-palms, and reddish in colour. They wear neither coat nor *kaftan*, but each man carried a cape which covers one half of his body, leaving one hand free. No one is ever parted from his axe, sword, and knife. Their swords are Frankish in design, broad, flat, and fluted. Each man has a number of trees, figures, and the like from the finger-nails to the neck. Each woman carries on her bosom a container made of iron, silver, copper, or gold—its size and substance depending on her man's wealth. Attached to the container is a ring carrying her knife which is also tied to her bosom. Round her neck she wears gold or silver rings: when a man collects 10,000 dirhams he gives his wife a neck-ring, when he has 20,000 he gives two rings, and so the wife gets a new ring for each 10,000 dirhams added to the husband's wealth. One woman often has many neck-rings. Their finest ornament is the green clay-pearl on the ships. To provide this they go to great trouble; they buy one pearl for a dirham and combine the pearls into necklaces for their women.

Selection from Ibn Fadlan, *Description of the Russian Vikings,* (921–922), in J. Brondsted, *The Vikings,* trans. E. Bannister Good, Penguin Books, Harmondsworth, Middlesex, U.K., 1960.

scorpions and venomous snakes of all kinds. They were equipped with fine quivers and polished, shining yellow bows and strong spears. They wore heavy coats of mail of double refined iron and carried stout swords.

"On the other side were the brave Irishmen—the lions, wolfhounds and hawks of Ireland. They had spears and shields, broad axes and swords. They wore golden crested helmets and fine cloth tunics and shirts of many colours.

"When the battle began, Brian had his cushions spread upon the ground, opened his prayer book, put his hands together and prayed. The fighting continued from sunrise to sunset. . . . At the end of the day, the Irish gathered themselves for one last great effort and swept the Vikings from the field. In the excitement, the King's guards rushed off and joined in the killing.

"Then, three Vikings led by Earl Brodir approached the King. Brian arose and unsheathed his great two-handed sword. Brodir carried a gleaming battleaxe in his hand. He passed Brian without noticing him, but one of his men called out, 'This is the High King.' 'No,' said Earl Brodir, 'no, that is not he, but a noble priest.' 'By your leave,' insisted the soldier, 'that is Brian the High King.' At that, Brian struck Brodir with his sword and cut off his left leg and right foot. At the very same moment, the Viking dealt Brian a blow with his axe which cut off the King's head. Both fell dead to the ground."

The Viking Legacy

What had the Viking peoples achieved? Traditionally, historians have followed contemporary chroniclers and described them as barbarians who robbed, raped and murdered their way across Europe, wantonly destroying fine buildings and beautiful works of art. The Vikings did these things, but so did the other Europeans when they were fighting among themselves. What marked the Vikings out for special treatment by the chroniclers was their paganism.

On the credit side, the Vikings stimulated trade wherever they went and founded or developed thriving towns. Often, they taught the local people new skills like shipbuilding and coin making. The Vikings developed a distinctive art style, as anyone who looks at their swords, wood carvings and metal work can see. They produced a fine heroic literature—the Sagas—which forms part of our cultural heritage in the West.

Even their attacks had some value, since they forced their victims to stand together. For example, the Viking raids provided the stimulus for the conquest of England by the kings of Wessex and for the unification of the Slav tribes by the Rus.

Lastly, wherever they settled, they kept alive their own sense of personal freedom—when the Franks asked the Vikings who their leader was, they answered proudly, "We have no lord, we are all equal."

For two and a half centuries, the Vikings had terrorized Europe, But now people suddenly asked:

What has become of the warrior?
What has become of the steed?
What has become of the seats at the banquet?
Where are the joys of the hall?
O for the bright cup.
O for the mailclad warrior.
O for the glory of the prince.
Now that time has passed away
And grown dark under the cover of night
As if it had never been.

Feudalism as the Basis of Social Order

Jeffrey L. Singman

During the Early Middle Ages, life was very insecure and unstable. Centralized political authority was weak, there was little law or law enforcement, and conflict among warrior nobles was common. In the following selection, historian Jeffrey L. Singman argues that in such an environment feudalism provided a solid basis of organization. Feudalism gave authority to local leaders, who were the only true sources of stability during the period.

Singman points out that feudalism was extremely complex and that it varied from place to place. Yet he shows that feudalism was organized around fairly straightforward relationships. On the one hand, subordinate nobles were granted fiefs in return for their loyal support to more powerful nobles. This allowed for local leadership in the form of feudal vassals. On the other hand, feudalism provided protection to the serfs who worked on a vassal's manorial landholding.

Jeffrey L. Singman is the author of a number of books, including *Daily Life in Chaucer's England*. He also works as a university teacher and museum curator.

Feudalism took shape in the vacuum of authority left by the collapse of the Roman Empire in western Europe. The empire in its heyday furnished Europe with a highly developed political and economic infrastructure: roads, coinage, defense, governmental stability. As the empire withdrew from the West, the infrastructure withered, and each locality was obliged to look to its own resources. During the early Mid-

Excerpted from Jeffrey L. Singman, *Daily Life in Medieval Europe*. Copyright © 1999 Jeffrey L. Singman. Reprinted with permission from Greenwood Publishing Group, Inc., Westport, CT.

dle Ages, society rebuilt itself in response to the new political realities, and new systems of social organization evolved to replace those once provided by Rome. Feudalism emerged as a viable social framework that could function even in a relatively anarchic environment.

The most important factors in the feudal equation were land and military power. The two were closely interdependent, since those who had military power could assert and maintain control over land, while those who controlled land could amass the wealth needed to support military power. The emphasis on land reflected the low yield of agricultural produce to agricultural labor, which required nine-tenths of the population to be engaged in farming. It was also a natural result of the limited infrastructure for industry and trade. Although commerce came to play an increasingly important role in the economy of the High Middle Ages, land remained the greatest and most reliable source of wealth. The importance of military power in feudalism was a response to the weakness of governmental authority. After the collapse of the empire, western Europe could no longer look to the legions of Rome to ward off raids or invasions from without, or to keep the peace within. The advantage lay with those who could amass significant local military forces.

Personal Relationships Were the Basis of Feudalism

In the absence of centralized governmental authority, people look to personal relationships to bind society together. Feudalism evolved as a hierarchical system of personal relationships in which land and military power were the principal commodities exchanged. An individual with military power to offer gave his services to a feudal lord. The lord in turn secured his subordinate in the possession of the land that financed his military service. The feudal subordinate was called a vassal, and the vassal's land was termed a fee or fief (*feudum* in Latin, which is the source of the term feudal). A vassal who held a great deal of land might in turn grant fiefs to his own feudal tenants, who helped him fulfill his military obligations to his lord. Long-term stability was provided by the principle of heredity, as the feudal relationships between individuals were extended to apply to their heirs.

Feudal landholding lay somewhere between modern tenancy and ownership. The holder was considered the tenant rather than the owner of the holding. In principle, the lord might grant the fief at his will whenever it became empty. In practice, fiefs were treated as permanent and hereditary property, granted by the lord to the heir when the holder died, and only falling empty if there was no heir, or if the holder was forcefully dispossessed. Tenants regularly sold their tenancies, although the lord's permission had to be sought for the transaction. Heritability was advantageous for both lord and vassal, allowing the vassal to pass the property on to his heirs, and providing stability for the lord.

Servant   Pope of Rome   King   German noblewomen   German middle-class
                                                                              woman

Feudal society was comprised of the aristocracy who managed the government and the military and of the commoners who provided most of the labor.

The feudal transaction was more than a bartering of land for military service. The feudal tenant held some measure of legal jurisdiction and political authority over his holding and subtenants. At the same time, his status as a vassal involved more than just military service. The vassal did homage to the lord, symbolizing his status as his lord's man, owing him generalized loyalty and political support, while the lord in turn promised his patronage.

The king was the supreme feudal power in a kingdom. In theory, he was the owner and ruler of all the land, and delegated his authority to his tenants. In practice, his authority was often subject to challenge from his great lords, who together could wield military power comparable to his own. Not all land was held from a king or feudal lord. Some was held as inalienable property, called an allod. The holder of an allod might owe some form of allegiance to a suzerain (superior feudal lord). Suzerainty was a looser form of overlordship than sovereignty: the vassal owed homage to the lord, but because his feudal holding was not considered dependent on that relationship, homage was harder to enforce. Allods were not a feature of English feudalism, but they existed in France and were common in Germany.

Although historians sometimes speak of "the feudal system," feudalism was far from systematic. It evolved locally in response to local situations, and varied enormously from place to place. If a system can be perceived, it is because of shared circumstances, and because there was a degree of cultural contact and common cultural inheritance. Feudalism was complex, and the details varied greatly. Large landholdings were rarely solid blocks of territory, but scattered patchworks of feudal lands. Military service was commonly for forty days in the year, but it could be longer or shorter. The basic unit of feudal responsibility was the knight's service, the duty to provide a single mounted knight to serve one's lord. The exact number of services owed varied from fief to fief, depending partly on the value of the land, but also on the historical traditions associated with the holding. The distribution of power shifted over time, making new demands possible and old customs unenforceable, and in time these temporary shifts could themselves become established customs.

The Status of Serfs

Feudal society was based on a fundamental distinction between the aristocracy, whose function was military and governmental, and the commoners, the 98 percent of the population whose role it was to labor. Like the aristocracy, commoners inherited their status from their parents. Most were rural workers, living under the manorial system that mirrored many of the structures of the feudal hierarchy. The manor was the smallest unit of feudal landholding, typically a few hundred acres. It was essentially a holding sufficient to support an aristocratic household, including its most important feudal element, the knight. The manor lord parceled out some portion of his land to peasant tenants, keeping the rest in his own hands as demesne land to be cultivated for his own benefit. Like feudal vassals, the peasants provided service in exchange for their land, in this case labor service that the lord used to cultivate his demesne.

In addition, the lord exercised legal and governmental authority over the manor peasants. The nature of this jurisdiction depended on each peasant's personal status. In general, the medieval commoner was classed as free or unfree. Like other forms of personal status in the Middle Ages, freedom and unfreedom were inherited. People born of unfree parents were unfree themselves. In mixed unions, the customs varied, but commonly, legitimate children inherited their father's status, illegitimate ones their mother's. Unfree peasants, also called serfs or villeins, were personally subject to their manor lord in a manner that served to guarantee him a stable supply of labor: the serf was obliged to provide certain labor services for the lord, and he had to have the lord's permission to move away from the manor.

The institution of serfdom had some of its roots in the older practice of slavery, and the serf's status was in some ways akin to that of a slave. By the High Middle Ages, it was no longer considered appropriate for Christians to own other Christians as slaves, and true slavery persisted only at the margins of Europe where Christians were in contact with non-Christian societies. Serfdom, meanwhile, had been shaped by centuries of customs that tended to ease some of the serf's disadvantages, so that it would be misleading to equate serfdom with slavery. Serfs owed services to their lord, but these were limited by custom. A serf could be bought and sold, but the buyer acquired only the lord's traditional rights over the serf, not complete ownership. A serf's personal property in theory belonged to the lord, but in practice lords only collected traditional rents, fees, and fines from their serfs.

The idea of freedom and unfreedom was part of the shared heritage of medieval European cultures, dating back to ancient times, but its local manifestations in the Middle Ages were complex. There was a wide variety of local traditions and a spectrum of degrees of servitude. Even a free peasant might owe labor services, while not all serfs were subject to the full obligations of serfdom. There was a gray area in the middle where the categories of free and unfree were hard to apply. In parts of Europe, there were even quasi-aristocratic serfs known to historians as ministerials. The ministerials were descended from serfs who had served their lords as soldiers or administrators. Because of their ancestors' prestigious and influential work, their heirs enjoyed a certain aristocratic status that entitled them to hold feudal fiefs and become knights, yet they remained technically unfree. Ministerials were unknown in England, but they existed in France and were common in Germany and the Low Countries; in some parts of Germany, a majority of the knights were of unfree origin. . . .

The feudal and manorial hierarchy were defined by the aristocracy who were its principal beneficiaries. It is less clear how ordinary commoners perceived the social structure, since their perspective is generally missing from the written record. To some degree, they were participants in the feudal structure, yielding labor and taxes to their feudal lords, taking an active part in manorial institutions such as the manor court, and providing officers for the enforcement of the lord's manorial rights. It is far from certain, however, that the official distinctions between aristocrat and commoner or free and unfree were as important to the peasant as they were to his manor lord. Regardless of the serfs' resentment of their status, the distinction between serf and free commoner does not seem to have played a role in determining social status among commoners, and manorial records are full of small acts of resistance to the lord's authority. In the day-to-day life of the medieval commoner, relationships within the local community probably mattered more than the official feudal hierarchy.

Warriors and Fiefs

Sidney Painter

During the Early Middle Ages western Europe was dominated, aside from the leaders of the Roman Catholic
Church, by a warrior nobility. This warrior nobility had
evolved from the clan leaders of the Germanic tribes, and
still guided their kingdoms politically and militarily. During and after the Carolingian Era of the eighth and ninth
centuries, this warrior nobility was organized into a social
and political system known as feudalism.

According to Sidney Painter in the following excerpt,
feudalism grew out of the practice by which powerful nobles gave grants of land, or fiefs, to warriors who supported them. These fiefs were also known as benefices. A
warrior who was granted a fief was considered a vassal of
his lord, and was expected to support him in war. In addition, a vassal was required to pay homage to his lord,
which meant providing service in a number of ways, from
advice to money.

Painter argues, however, that feudalism and feudal relationships helped keep Europe in an almost chronic state of
war. Disputes over fiefs were frequent, success in war was
the basis for granting or withholding fiefs, and warrior
nobles generally chose to settle their arguments on the
battlefield.

Sidney Painter was professor of medieval history at
Johns Hopkins University.

Feudalism was the most important of the few original cre-
ations of the period known to us as the Middle Ages. The
product of an age of anarchy lying under the spectre of Imperial Rome, it became a fundamental element of the politi-

Excerpted from Sidney Painter, "Feudalism and Western Civilization," in *Feudalism and Liberty: Articles and Addresses of Sidney Painter*, edited by Fred A. Cazel Jr.
Copyright © 1961 The Johns Hopkins University Press. Reprinted with permission from The Johns Hopkins University Press.

cal institutions of Western Europe. Long after the disappearance of feudalism as a living political system, its traditions deeply affected the accepted political ideas of this region and inhibited the development of both absolutist government and nationalism. In it lay the foundations of the Anglo-American conception of government which has played so important a part in the modern world.

Feudalism Was Built Around the Landholdings of Warriors

Feudal institutions were restricted to a particular class of society—the warrior aristocracy. This class created for itself a set, or perhaps one should say several sets, of ethical ideas which were in accord with the requirements of the feudal environment. Their propagation was the work of writers and reciters who embodied them in an extensive literature intended to be heard rather than read. These ideas long outlasted the class that originated them and are still an important part of our social heritage. Our conception of a gentleman and of the ideal state of matrimony are largely based on the ethical ideas of the feudal class. And the literature in which they were expressed, especially the Arthurian legends, still stirs the imagination of writers of both prose and poetry.

The term feudal has a curious and complicated history. All the Germanic languages had a word for cattle. As cattle were the only moveable goods of any importance among the early Germans, these words soon took the wider meaning of chattels. The Gallo-Roman language of the West Frankish state adopted such a term from the Franks and made it into "fie" or "fief." In the tenth century we find it used for arms, clothing, horses, and food. The man of wealth who kept a warrior in his household supplied him with these things. Hence when he decided to give the warrior land to support him, what was then called a "benefice," some called this land a fief. For a while we find such expressions as "a benefice vulgarly called a fief" and then the word "fief" triumphed and "benefice" disappeared.

"Fief" became "feudum" in Latin. In the seventeenth century "féodale" and "feudal" appear in France and England respectively as legal terms to refer to anything connected with fiefs and fiefholders—the mediaeval nobles and their lands. In the eighteenth century the meaning of these words was extended to cover the relations between the fief-holder and the non-noble peasants who tilled his fief. This usage appears in full force in 1789 in the famous decree of the National Assembly abolishing the "régime féodale.". . .

Charles Martel Gives Land to His Soldiers

In discussing the beginnings of feudalism one must distinguish between feudal institutions and a feudal system. Feudal institutions appeared in early Carolingian times. Charles Martel needed a reliable and effective military force to stabilize his power in the Frankish state and to check the inroads of such external foes as the Moslems and the Saxons. The economy of Western Europe had fallen to a point where there was little money in circulation. Charles could support soldiers only by giving them land and the labor to work it. The Frankish church had an immense amount of land—scholars have guessed that it held about one third of the land in the state. To get its land cultivated, the church had long used an institution called a benefice. A benefice was a grant of land for a fixed term, often for the grantee's lifetime, in return for certain services. Charles used church land to grant benefices to his warriors. But Charles wanted not merely soldiers but soldiers who would stick by him through thick and thin. Now from the time when they had left the dank forests of North Germany to enter Gaul the Frankish kings had had a band of chosen men bound to them by special oaths—their *comitatus* or trustee. Charles Martel combined this institution with the benefice. The men to whom he gave benefices swore to be ever faithful to him. As the term *vassus* was in common use for dependents of various kinds, Charles applied it to his new soldiers. They became *vassi dominici*, vassals of the lord.

The granting of benefices became a general practice in the Carolingian Empire. The kings gave them from church lands, from territories conquered from their neighbors such as the March of Barcelona, and from estates belonging to the crown. Great Frankish landowners copied the king and granted benefices from their proprietary lands, their allods.

Feudalism as a Source of Stability

As the Carolingian government decayed in the ninth and tenth centuries under the stress of internal strife and fierce attacks by Vikings, Moslems, and Magyars, the personal relationship between lord and vassal became one of the few stable elements in society. Though it never entirely replaced the far more ancient tie of kinship, it gradually gained priority over it. Hence there was a tendency for all political relationships to become feudal. The king's deputies in the various regions, the dukes and counts, became his vassals and their offices were considered to be benefices.

The early Carolingians—Charles Martel, Pepin, and Charlemagne—granted benefices and took them back at will. Their weaker successors undoubtedly found it extremely difficult to deprive an able warrior of his benefice. In fact, when a vassal died leaving a son who was an effective soldier, there was little point in attempting to prevent him from succeeding to his father's benefice. Thus while benefices were never recognized as hereditary during the Carolingian period, by the tenth century they usually were in practice when the heir was a male of full age. By the end of the eleventh century only the lord's right to a money payment called "relief," when the son succeeded his father, bore witness of earlier custom. Moreover, custom was beginning to demand that a lord safeguard the hereditary rights of a daughter or a son who was under age. The development of the principle of the hereditability of fiefs was obviously a most important stage in the history of feudalism. A temporary delegation of property or power had become an established proprietary right.

During the period when benefices or, as we shall now call them, fiefs were gradually becoming hereditary, another important change was taking place. In the ninth century most of the great landowners who had fiefs held them directly from the king—were, in short, the successors of the *vassi dominici*. But bit by bit the dukes and counts persuaded or forced the royal vassals in their territories to become their men. In 1025 Hugh IV de Lusignan was not quite sure whether he and his neighboring fief-holders were primarily vassals of the king or of the count of Poitou, but their successors were clearly the count's men. Thus there developed a feudal hierarchy on a territorial basis.

By the end of the ninth century feudal institutions were common in every part of the Frankish Empire except Saxony. In all probability a large percentage of the great landholders held benefices and were vassals. But these fief-holders usually had allodial lands as well, and in most cases they were more extensive than the fiefs. Moreover, there were many great men who held *only* allods*. At this point the history of the West and East Frankish states diverged sharply. The tenth and eleventh centuries saw the East Frankish state, modern Germany, ruled by strong kings who maintained their power and gave no encouragement to the development of a complete feudal system. But during this same period the West Frankish state, modern France, fell into almost complete anarchy. Every man who could afford the military equipment was a knight, and every knight's sword was turned against his neighbors. Public authority broke down completely, and feudal institutions were too scattered to take its place. Even if a count wanted to maintain order and could secure the obedience of his vassals, the great allodial holdings escaped all superior authority.

During the course of the eleventh, twelfth, and in some regions the thirteenth centuries, the dukes, counts, and barons of France gradually brought the allods within the system of fiefs. The process is not entirely clear to us. In some cases it was done by force of arms, in others by the grant of privileges, and in others by money payments. Thus by the eleventh century the dukes of Burgundy were strong enough to forbid anyone to build a castle on an allod in the counties they controlled. If a man wanted to build a fortress, he had to turn its site into a fief held of the duke. In the thirteenth

---

*Eds. note: An allod was land that was held independently, rather than a fief which had been granted by a lord.

century the Burgundian dukes were giving lump sums of money to holders of allods to persuade them to do homage for their allodial lands. The allod never entirely disappeared in France. Only in those countries where feudalism was introduced by a conqueror—England, Sicily, Palestine, and Greece—did the feudal system become complete and all embracing. But by 1200 Northern France was almost completely feudalized, and the feudal bond became a reasonably effective political cement.

The Knight on Horseback Was the Center of Feudal Relations

I can only describe the feudal *system* in the briefest possible manner. Its base was the fully armed warrior—the knight. He had a fief which consisted of enough land and labor to support him. When he received his fief, the knight did homage to a lord. The lord was bound to protect the knight, his family, and his fief. In return the knight was bound to be faithful to his lord and do him service. When the lord needed soldiers for war in the field or to garrison his castle, the knight had to appear in full armor. When the lord summoned his vassals to court, the knight was bound to attend. When a vassal died, his heir owed the lord a money payment called relief and the vassal was expected to aid the lord financially on certain occasions such as the wedding of his eldest daughter or the knighting of his eldest son. The rights and duties of lord and vassals were set in the lord's court—an assembly of vassals presided over by the lord. These definitions of rights and duties were feudal law or custom and differed from fief to fief. Thus for example two fiefs lying side by side might have entirely different laws governing inheritance.

The feudal system provided for military and political cooperation between members of the knightly class with the least possible restraint on individual liberty. A knight had certain definite personal obligations toward his lord and his own vassals. He had rather more vague ones toward other vassals of his lord. But toward all other men he was a free agent who could do what he pleased. Thus it was a serious offence for him to rape the daughter of his lord or of one of his own vassals, but he could rape anyone else's daughter with impunity if he was powerful enough to ignore the ire of her relatives. Outside the bounds of feudal custom, the vassal was unrestrained. And within the feudal class the system was completely democratic—custom was set and enforced by the vassals.

Trying to Prevent Feudal Violence

Since the feudal system seemed to encourage warfare, the church tried its best to control the damage by making declarations forbidding acts of violence against churches and the poor. "Anathema" means that anyone committing such an act might be excommunicated from the church.

Following the example of my predecessors, I, Gunbald, archbishop of Bordeaux, called together the bishops of my diocese in a synod at Charroux, . . . and we, assembled there in the name of God, made the following decrees:

1. Anathema against those who break into churches. If anyone breaks into or robs a church, he shall be anathema unless he makes satisfaction.

2. Anathema against those who rob the poor. If anyone robs a peasant or any other poor person of a sheep, ox, ass, cow, goat, or pig, he shall be anathema unless he makes satisfaction.

3. Anathema against those who injure clergymen. If anyone attacks, seizes, or beats a priest, deacon, or any other clergyman, who is not bearing arms (shield, sword, coat of mail, or helmet), but is going along peacefully or staying in the house, the sacrilegious person shall be excommunicated and cut off from the church, unless he makes satisfaction, or unless the bishop discovers that the clergyman brought it upon himself by his own fault.

Selection from *The Middle Ages Volume I: Sources of Medieval History*, 2nd edition, ed. Brian Tierney. New York: Alfred A. Knopf, 1970, p. 106.

Thus the feudal relationship was essentially a contract between lord and vassals which was defined and enforced by mutual agreement. The system operated in the same manner. It was assumed that lord and vassals had a common interest—the welfare of the fief. No lord was expected to make a serious decision, such as choosing a wife or going to war, without asking counsel of his vassals.

As a political system pure feudalism was little removed from anarchy. It assumed a more-or-less permanent state of war. While it provided machinery for the peaceful settling of most disputes, it did not *compel* men to settle their disputes peacefully. Thus if two knights quarrelled, they could always find a feudal court competent to hear the case, but if they preferred to wage war on each other, and they usually did, feudal custom did not hinder them. France in the eleventh and early twelfth centuries, and parts of Germany in the fourteenth and fifteenth, are prime examples of feudalism uncontrolled by public authority. In England from the beginning, in France after 1150, and in Germany before the downfall of the Hohenstaufen dynasty, royal authority based on the traditions of Germanic monarchy, mingled vaguely with those of Imperial Rome, curbed feudal anarchy to some extent. Because these kings ruled through a combination of royal and feudal institutions—were both kings and feudal suzerains—historians call them "feudal monarchs."

The Obligations of Feudal Vassals

Marc Bloch

In feudalism, nobles were arranged into a hierarchy of lords and vassals. The highest of all nobles, the one who held the most fiefs and commanded the loyalty of the most vassals, was generally king. Beneath him, his vassals, depending on their power and on the extent of their fiefs, might have many vassals of their own.

In the following selection, French medieval historian Marc Bloch describes the many obligations that feudal vassals held. Vassals were expected to serve their lords in war, as advisers and servants at court, and even financially. In turn, they were granted fiefs and given a certain degree of protection. Bloch argues, however, that the system generally worked in favor of the higher lords. For many vassals, there were more obligations than advantages.

Marc Bloch is thought to be among the greatest medieval historians. *Feudal Society*, from which this excerpt is taken, is considered to be the standard work on the subject.

'To serve' or (as it was sometimes put) 'to aid', and 'to protect' —it was in these very simple terms that the oldest texts summed up the mutual obligations of the armed retainer and his lord. Never was the bond felt to be stronger than in the period when its effects were thus stated in the vaguest and, consequently, the most comprehensive fashion. When we define something, do we not always impose limitations on it? It was inevitable, nevertheless, that the need to define the legal consequences of the contract of homage should be felt with increasing urgency, especially in so far as they affected

Excerpted from Marc Bloch, *Feudal Society*. Copyright © 1961 Routledge & Kegan Paul Ltd. Reprinted with permission from the University of Chicago Press.

the obligations of the subordinate. Once vassalage had emerged from the humble sphere of domestic loyalty, what vassal thenceforth would have regarded it as compatible with his dignity if it had been frankly stated, as in early times, that he was compelled 'to serve the lord in all manner of tasks which may be required of him'? Furthermore, could the lord continue to expect to have always at his beck and call persons who thenceforward—since they were for the most part settled on fiefs—lived at a distance from their master? . . .

A Feudal Vassal Was Bound to Fight for His Lord

The primary duty was, by definition, military service. The 'man of mouth and hands' was bound, first and foremost, to serve in person, on horseback and with full equipment. Nevertheless he rarely appeared alone. Apart from the fact that his own vassals, if he had any, would naturally gather under his banner and share his privileges and his prestige, custom sometimes required him to be attended by at least one or two squires. On the other hand there were as a rule no foot-soldiers in his contingent. Their rôle in battle was considered so unimportant and the difficulty of feeding fairly large bodies of men was so great that the leader of the feudal host contented himself with the peasant infantry furnished by his own estates or those of the churches of which he had officially constituted himself the protector. Frequently the vassal was also required to garrison the lord's castle, either during hostilities only, or—for a fortress could not remain unguarded—at any time, in rotation with his fellow-vassals. If he had a fortified house of his own, he was obliged to throw it open to his lord.

Gradually differences in rank and power, the development of inevitably divergent traditions, special agreements, and even abuses transformed into rights introduced innumerable variations into these obligations. This, in the long run, almost invariably tended to lighten them.

A serious problem arose from the hierarchical organization of vassalage. Since the vassal was at once subject and master, he would often have vassals of his own. The duty which required him to render aid to his lord to the utmost of his ability might be thought to oblige him to join the lord's army, together with the entire body of his dependants. Custom, however, at an early date authorized him to bring with him only a stated number of followers; the figure was fixed once and for all, and might be much less than the number he employed in his own wars. Take the case, towards the end of the eleventh century, of the bishop of Bayeux. More than a hundred knights owed him military service, but he was bound to provide only twenty of them for the duke of Normandy, his immediate lord. Moreover, if the duke demanded the help of the prelate in the name of the king of France (of whom Normandy was held as a fief) the number was reduced to ten. This fining down of the military obligation towards the summit, which the Plantagenet kings of England in the twelfth century tried without much success to arrest, was undoubtedly one of the principal causes of the final failure of vassalage as a means of defence or conquest in the hands of governments.

It was the chief desire of vassals both great and small not to be held to an indefinite period of military service. But neither the traditions of the Carolingian state nor the earliest usages of vassalage offered direct precedents for limiting its duration. Both the subject and the household warrior remained under arms as long as their presence seemed necessary to king or chief. The old Germanic customs, on the other hand, had widely employed a sort of standard period fixed at forty days or, as they said earlier, forty nights. This not only regulated many forms of procedure; Frankish military legislation itself had adopted forty days as the period of rest to which the levies were entitled between two mobilizations. This traditional period, which came naturally to mind, provided from the end of the eleventh century the normal standard for the obligation imposed on the vassals; on the expiration of forty days they were free to return home, usually for the rest of the year. It is true that they fairly frequently remained with the army, and certain 'customs' even sought to make this prolongation of the period of service compulsory, though only on condition that the lord bore the expense and paid wages to the vassal. The fief, once the stipend of the armed 'satellite', had so far ceased to fulfil its original purpose that it was necessary to supplement it by other remuneration.

Kings and Their Courts

It was not only for war that the lord summoned his vassals. In peacetime, they constituted his 'court', which he convoked in solemn session at more or less regular intervals, coinciding as a rule with the principal liturgical feasts. It was by turns a court of law, a council which the master was required by the political conceptions of the time to consult on all serious matters, and a ceremonial parade of rank and power. Could a chief have a more striking manifestation of his prestige or a more delightful way of reminding himself of it than to appear in public surrounded by a multitude of dependants, some of whom were themselves men of high rank, and to get them to perform publicly those gestures of deference—by acting as squire, cup-bearer or steward—to which an age susceptible to visible things attached great symbolic value?

The splendour of these courts, 'full, marvellous and great', has been naively exaggerated by the epic poems, in which they are frequent backgrounds to the action. While the glories of the ceremonial gatherings graced by the presence of crowned kings were greatly magnified, the poets even added gratuitous splendours to the modest courts convoked by barons of medium or lesser rank. Nevertheless, we know from the most reliable sources that much legal business was dealt with in these assemblies; that the most brilliant of them were marked by much ceremonial display and attracted—in addition to those who normally attended—a mixed crowd of adventurers, mountebanks and even pickpockets; and that the lord was required by usage as well as by his acknowledged interest, to distribute to his men on these occasions those gifts of horses, arms, and vestments which were at once the guarantee of their fealty and the symbol of their subordination. We know, moreover, that the presence of the vassals—each, as the abbot of Saint-Riquier prescribed, 'carefully arrayed in accordance with his rank'—was always expressly required. According to the *Usages of*

Barcelona, the count, when he holds court, must 'render justice . . . give help to the oppressed . . . announce mealtimes with trumpets so that nobles and others of lesser rank may participate; he must distribute cloaks to his chief vassals; make arrangements for the expedition which will harry the lands of Spain; and create new knights'. At a lower level of the social hierarchy, a petty knight of Picardy, acknowledging himself in 1210 the liegeman of the vidame of Amiens, promised him, in the same breath, military aid for a period of six months and 'to come, when I am required to do so, to the feast given by the said vidame, staying there, with my wife, at my own expense, for eight days'.

A Lord's Possible Crimes Against His Vassals

As the feudal system took hold during the Carolingian era of the eighth and ninth centuries, the Frankish kings made declarations such as this one. It describes which acts would allow a vassal freedom from obligations to his lord.

If anyone shall wish to leave his lord (*seniorem*), and is able to prove against him one of these crimes, that is, in the first place, if the lord has wished to reduce him unjustly into servitude; in the second place, if he has taken counsel against his life; in the third place, if the lord has committed adultery with the wife of his vassal; in the fourth place, if he has wilfully attacked him with a drawn sword; in the fifth place, if the lord has been able to bring defence to his vassal after he has commended his hands to him, and has not done so; it is allowed to the vassal to leave him. If the lord has perpetrated anything against the vassal in these five points it is allowed the vassal to leave him.

Selection from *The Middle Ages Volume I: Sources of Medieval History*, 2nd edition, ed. Brian Tierney. New York: Alfred A. Knopf, 1970, p. 106.

This last example (together with many others) shows how court service, like military service, was gradually regulated and limited—though it is true that the attitude of the vassals towards the two obligations was not altogether the same.

Military service was an obligation and little else, but attendance at court carried with it many advantages: gifts from one's lord, a groaning board and a share in the exercise of authority. The vassals were, therefore, much less eager to be relieved of court service than of military service. Till the end of the feudal era these assemblies compensated in some measure for the separation of lord and vassal resulting from the grant of a fief; they helped to maintain the personal contact without which a human tie can scarcely exist.

Feudal Service Might Take the Form of Payment

The vassal was bound by his fealty to 'render aid' to his lord in all things, and it was taken for granted that this meant placing his sword and his counsel at his lord's disposal. But there came a time when he was expected to make his purse available as well. No institution reveals better than this financial obligation the deep-seated unity of the system of dependence on which feudal society was built. Whoever owed obedience was obliged to give financial help to his chief or master in case of need: the serf, the so-called 'free' tenant of a manor, the subject of a king, and finally the vassal. The very terms applied to the contributions which the lord was thus authorized to demand from his men were, at least in French feudal law, identical regardless of who paid them. . . .

Inevitably it happened from time to time that the obligation of military service was not carried out. The lord thereupon claimed a fine or compensation; occasionally the vassal offered it in advance. This was called 'service', in conformity with the linguistic convention whereby the payment of compensation was frequently given the name of the obligation which it extinguished; in France it was sometimes known as *taille de l'ost*. These dispensations for a cash payment were not in fact widely practised except in the case of two categories of fiefs: those which had fallen into the hands of religious communities, who were unable to bear arms; and those held directly of the great monarchies, which were adept at turning to their own financial profit the inadequacies of the system of vassal recruitment. For the majority of feudal tenements, the duty of military service from the thirteenth century onward merely became less and less exacting, without any tax being imposed in its place. Even the pecuniary aids frequently fell into desuetude in the end. The fief had ceased to procure good servants: neither did it long remain a fruitful source of revenue.

Custom in most cases did not require of the lord any verbal or written agreement corresponding to the oath of the vassal. Such pledges on the lord's part appeared only at a later date and always remained exceptional. There was no opportunity, therefore, to define the obligations of the chief in as much detail as those of the subordinate. A duty of protection, moreover, did not lend itself so well as services to such precise definition. The vassal was to be defended by his lord 'towards and against all men who may live and die'; first and foremost in his person, but also in his property and more especially in his fiefs. Furthermore he expected from this protector—who had become . . . a judge—good and speedy justice. In addition, there were the imponderable but nevertheless precious advantages which accrued, rightly or wrongly, from the patronage of a powerful man in a highly anarchic society. All these advantages were prized; nevertheless in the long run the vassal's obligations outweighed the benefits he received. As remuneration for service, the fief had originally redressed the balance, but when by reason of its transformation into a patrimonial property its original function was lost sight of, the inequality of the obligations seemed all the more flagrant, and those who suffered from it were all the more anxious to limit their burden.

The Serfs of the Manor

Joseph Dahmus

In the following selection, Joseph Dahmus points out that
feudal Europe consisted mostly of agricultural peasants
rather than warrior nobles. Peasants were expected to perform the labor that supported the nobility and the church;
in return they were governed and protected.

Peasants in medieval Europe were organized into
manorial villages, which were small communities centered
around the manor houses of nobles and surrounded by
agricultural land. According to Dahmus, most of the peasants in manorial villages were not free; they were serfs.

Like their lords, feudal serfs were bound by obligations
and expectations. Frequently they were held by long-term
leases on their land. These leases were passed down from
father to son. In addition, serfs were required to work the
land held by the lord of the manor. Finally, serfs were not
always free to leave the land on which they lived and
worked, although, as Dahmus suggests, few would have
wanted to. Dahmus claims, however, that serfs were not
slaves in that they had certain rights and freedoms.

Popular historian Joseph Dahmus is the author of eight
books on the Middle Ages, including *Seven Medieval Kings*
and *Seven Medieval Queens*.

Alongside the knight and feudal aristocracy that dominated
western Europe during the feudal age was the mass of peasantry who made up the greater part of its population. The
one class ruled society and provided it protection; the second
group labored with its hands to furnish the food and services
the landowning class required to perform its work. Feudal
society had need of both classes to maintain itself, and for

that reason God had so ordered. "It is seemly," wrote the saintly Ramón Lull, "that men should plow and dig and work hard that the earth may yield the fruits from which the knight and his horse will live; and that the knight who rides and does a lord's work should get his wealth from the things on which his men are to spend much toil and fatigue."

Peasants had, of course, existed long before the feudal age, and they would continue to constitute the largest group in society long after strong kings had deprived the feudal aristocracy of its authority and purpose. The kind of toil, too, that the peasant performed, chiefly that of working the soil in order to raise food, did not alter appreciably during the feudal age to justify setting his group off from the husbandmen of preceding and of subsequent centuries. Nevertheless, the peculiar term "serf" by which this peasant is traditionally known during the feudal age suggests that he was not just another farmer. Circumstances were present, such as those affecting his relationship to his lord for instance, that gave him a distinctly different character. In many respects his status, rights, and obligations bore strong resemblance to those of his aristocratic superiors, even though an impassable barrier marked off the one class from the other. Both knight and serf were typical of the feudal age.

Most People Were Peasants, Not Knights

Two features of peasant life during the feudal age that come readily to mind bore no immediate relationship to the presence of a feudal aristocracy. One was the large percentage of people who lived as peasants in this feudal period; a second, the tendency of these peasants to live together in villages. When Ramón Lull wrote of the men who "spend much toil and fatigue," he was probably speaking of more than 90 per cent of the population of western Europe. The percentage in Italy where there were towns, would be lower; in England it might be higher. The Domesday Book survey which William the Conqueror ordered in 1086 revealed more than 95 per cent of England's population living in the country and drawing its livelihood from the soil. Seldom in recorded history has so large a percentage of an area's population pursued nonpastoral agriculture.

More unique was the practice for peasants, during this age, of living together in villages and hamlets, rather than in individual homesteads scattered about the countryside. In the larger villages several hundred families might be gathered together; in the hamlets no more than a score. Where the community was a large one, it might actually represent two or more manors belonging to as many different lords. Here in this custom of peasants living together there is evident some link with feudalism, since the manorial village or manor was most common in the most highly feudalized parts of western Europe. In those areas, as we shall note, agriculture was also most highly developed. Why peasants chose to live together in villages may require no explanation beyond their need for protection. As we have seen, that was the crying need of the time, and where better to assure oneself of the lord's protection than living in the shadow of his fortified manor house or castle.

The Nature of the Manorial Village

The organization of the economic and social life of the peasantry about the village and the isolation of this community from other villages and towns introduces another feature of manorial life during the feudal period which was probably unique. The manor during that period was a self-sufficient institution. Because of the absence of roads and the great difficulty and danger involved in moving about, the peasant village depended upon its own resources to satisfy its need for food and services. What it required to exist, it raised or produced, and what it could not produce, it normally did without. Because of the prevalence of this agricultural economy throughout the area, even the presence of roads would not have greatly altered the situation since the peasants of a wide region ordinarily raised the same kind of crops. The typical peasant community lived a life all its own. The lord would provide it some connection with the outside world, or an occasional pilgrim, the bishop of the diocese, or a representative of the crown. Other visitors—marauders and enemies—the lord of the manor would hopefully drive off.

The most unusual feature of the manorial village, from point of view of the modern world, was the unfree status of the greater number of its inhabitants and their complete dependence upon their local lord. The great majority of the peasants could not leave the community without the lord's permission; they owed him obligations which suggested a servile status; in the most highly feudalized parts of Europe they had, indeed, no existence apart from their lord. They were dependent upon him for justice and protection, for the use of his land, even for the spiritual services of a priest whom he might appoint. So much was he their lord, that the authority of the king and of the church, when this reached them, did so through his permission. . . .

One may trace the other principal source of the manor's unfree population to the troubled conditions of the sixth, seventh, and eighth centuries. As noted above in the discussion of the origins of feudalism, those were centuries when men sought protection. To the lord who might furnish them protection, many men were willing to surrender ownership of their lands and their personal freedom as well. Everywhere men were commending themselves. The more fortunate, generally those who had more to offer, might serve their lord in some military or administrative capacity. The humbler sort, simple tillers of the soil, would remain farmers. They would continue at the same occupation as before, but now on land which belonged to the lord and on terms that left them unfree. In many instances, these unfree peasants had never had the opportunity to choose between freedom and the surrender of that freedom for protection. A powerful lord might simply have taken over control of them and their village. Whatever the circumstances, the end was the same. They now had the status of serfs.

Few People Were Free

Now, while the great majority of villagers during the feudal period were unfree, there were some who dwelt in the village who were free. These would include the lord of the manor, for instance, and his family, who might spend extended periods in the "big house" on the hill. How many weeks or months they spent in the village would depend upon a number of circumstances: the comfortableness of the manor house, the depth of its larder, the friendliness of the villagers, the abundance of game, the proximity to danger from attack, and the number of manors the lord might possess. In the course of the year, he would normally spend some time in each of his manors, if for no other reason, in order to consume the stores his serfs had provided him. However great the amount of time he spent at any one manor, he never ceased being something of an outsider, a member of the second estate as it came to be called, not of the third to which the unfree villagers belonged.

Another free man who lived in the village and who was not a member of the third estate of the commoners was the priest. His clerical rank placed him with the first estate, that is, with the group which concerned itself with spiritual matters. To this class the Middle Ages granted precedence, at least officially. By birth, however, and culture the village priest did not differ appreciably from the serfs among whom he labored. What may have explained his rise above that class was perhaps his intelligence as a boy which had attracted the attention of an earlier "parson" who had ministered to that community. This man taught him a little Latin, brought him to the attention of the lord, who in turn had the bishop ordain him and assign him to the village. The house that the priest occupied in the village was not different from the others, neither was his fare, and he might work his acres when they worked theirs. If his store of erudition was meager, neither the lord nor the villagers would have been apt to notice since theirs was no higher. Rarely does any great gulf separate the literacy or, for that matter, the morality of a native clergy from that of the people it serves.

Apart from the lord of the manor and the priest, there might be other freemen living in the village. These would be commoners, members of the third estate, of the class that constituted the bulk of the manor's population. By some fortunate circumstance, they had never surrendered nor been deprived of their freedom. That their number was small, given the turbulent conditions of the feudal age, is understandable. If the manor's population included very few slaves, that is also easy to understand. What services the lord of the manor required, he could demand of his serfs; so why have slaves in his household whose food and shelter he would be expected to provide?

Serfs and Their Obligations

This centers attention on the last group, the great mass of serfs, the unfree, who made up most of the population of the manor. In terms of rights and obligations, they stood between the minority of freemen who were above them and the few slaves who were beneath. What these rights and obligations might be varied with province and century, and, above all, with the arrangement entered in between the individual lord and villager. The latter might be a free villein, that is, one who paid a rental yet could not leave the village without the lord's permission. He might be a cottar, own only a cottage, and have no acres either of his own nor any others to rent, and limited for his livelihood to what he could earn working as a day laborer for his fellow serfs or for the lord. The scholar who attempts to spell out in precise terms the rights and obligations of each rank between the free villein and cottar and to note how these not only might differ from province to province but how they underwent constant change, will find that he has buried both himself and his reader in hopeless confusion. Suffice it to say that by the close of the twelfth century, the common terms of serf and villein, which were applied to the great majority of these villagers, had come to be largely synonymous.

The word "serf" is derived from the Latin *servus* which in classical times meant either slave or servant. The medieval serf was no slave even though two circumstances have left many people the impression that he was. One circumstance was the fact that he worked the demesne of the lord. The demesne was that part of the manorial lands, frequently one-third, which the lord kept for himself. The other circumstance was the serf's inability to leave the manor. To a modern generation both circumstances connote slavery; to the Middle Ages they did not.

The serf worked the land of his lord because he had none of his own. He had surrendered his farm to his lord in return for the latter's protection. What the serf continued to do, however, was to retain use (not ownership) of his land, as did the lord's other serfs. So while they worked the acres they had been permitted to use for themselves, they also worked the lords demesne, partly to compensate him for the protection he was affording them, partly as a kind of rental for the acres which they were using for themselves. Had land possessed capitalistic value in the feudal age and had the serf money in sufficient quantity, he might have paid this rent in coin rather than labor. That would have saved modern students from the pitfall into which many of them have fallen in assuming the serf's labor charge made him a slave.

The other circumstance that leads some readers to ascribe a slave status to the serf, namely, his inability to leave the manor, no more denoted a servile condition than the labor rent he paid. One might ask first, why should the serf wish to leave the manor if he had just turned over his lands to the lord in return for his protection? The conclusion is, therefore, inevitable that the serf (tenant, the man who commended himself) had lived for a number of generations on the lord's lands before the thought of leaving had ever occurred to him. By the time it did, in the late eleventh century for instance, tradition had already established the rule that he was not to leave the manor. By that time, too, the lord had come to consider the serf as much a physical asset as the acres he worked, since without men to work the land the latter would have been of no value. The modern student should also keep in mind that mobility and freedom did not bear the same relationship in the Middle Ages as they may today. One last observation: if the serf did decide to leave the manor, he could flee to a distant town without great difficulty in a country such as France where the authority of the local lord lapsed at the confines of his land and where no effectual royal authority existed prior to the thirteenth century which might have worked to return the serf whence he had come. In England it would have been difficult to flee by the twelfth century, although custom then prescribed that a lord could not reclaim a serf who had been away for a year and a day.

Serfs Were Not Slaves

The point of this discussion is to present the status of the serf as fundamentally different from that of the slave despite the serf's inability to leave the manor and the obligation upon him to work the acres of his lord. This last, called the *corvée*, represented the serf's heaviest burden. The lord might require two days of his time one week, three another, or even four. During the summer the serf spent his time in the fields; during the winter, at such tasks as repairing roads and walls, or cutting and transporting wood. Some serfs might be occupied summer and winter in the mill or smithy or about the manor house. At the peak of the harvest season, the serf could expect to put in a few extra days, called boon work, when his older children and his wife might join him. (Medieval women usually helped with the harvest and with the chores around the barn.) While the *corvée* might appear excessive, and the serf was sure it was, the days he put in working for his lord did not normally exceed half-days, while boon work was not without its pleasant features. The entire community joined together in bringing in the harvest, while the lord provided most of the food and drink from his own larder. Many serfs never ate white bread except on such occasions, nor could their vintage match that of the lord.

The serf bore a variety of charges in addition to the *corvée* that kept reminding him he was a serf and that all he possessed, including his land, belonged ultimately to his lord. Relatively common was the tallage (taille), which was ordinarily a tax on property and, like most taxes, paid in kind. The first tallage had been a gift, then became a regular charge, not an uncommon development in the Middle Ages when the temptation was strong to proclaim what was done once, surely twice, as custom. In France the taille gradually replaced the labor charge *(corvée)* since the seigneur in that country had parceled out most of his demesne among his serfs by the thirteenth century. The serf also paid a head tax, a *formariage* when his daughter married off the manor, and his family a mortuary gift [heriot] when he died. This was often a heavy payment and, in this respect at least, paralleled the relief paid by the vassal. In the case of the serf, the heriot might constitute his most precious chattel. The serf also paid a tithe to the church (unless the lord had appropriated this), one fourth of which was to go to the bishop, part to maintain the church building, part for the priest, and part for charity.

Though the serf complained about the heavy burden his lord laid upon him in taxes and prestations, and in his somber moments might have likened his status to that of a slave, he did possess important rights which furnished him a substantially higher status. He had the right to work the acres of his father (after paying the mortuary gift) and, in proportion to the extent of these acres, to share the use of the pasture lands, the commons, and the forest. The lord could not expel him from the manor or deprive him of his home. The serf had both the duty and privilege of attending the manorial court which settled disputes, property claims, and minor infractions of the peace and moral tranquillity of the village. If a senior member of the court, he would advise with others in matters that pertained to the well-being of the community. He also had the right to marry, to raise a family, and to worship. And he ordinarily did no field work on Sundays and holydays.

Appendix of Documents

Document 1: A Glorification of Constantine

Constantine, Roman emperor from 306 to 337, not only established a new imperial capital at Constantinople, he was the first Christian emperor, having accepted baptism before his death. Constantine's friend, Eusebius, Bishop of Caesarea, claimed that the emperor was as godly as the ancient prophets and the early Christians.

Mankind, devising some consolation for the frail and precarious duration of human life, have thought by the erection of monuments to glorify the memories of their ancestors with immortal honors. Some have employed the vivid delineations and colors of painting; some have carved statues from lifeless blocks of wood; while others, by engraving their inscriptions deep on tablets and monuments, have thought to transmit the virtues of those whom they honored to perpetual remembrance. All these indeed are perishable, and consumed by the lapse of time, being representations of the corruptible body, and not expressing the image of the immortal soul. And yet these seemed sufficient to those who had no well-grounded hope of happiness after the termination of this mortal life. But God, that God, I say, who is the common Saviour of all, having treasured up with himself, for those who love godliness, greater blessings than human thought has conceived, gives the earnest and first-fruits of future rewards even here, assuring in some sort immortal hopes to mortal eyes. The ancient oracles of the prophets, delivered to us in the Scripture, declare this; the lives of pious men, who shone in old time with every virtue, bear witness to posterity of the same; and our own days prove it to be true, wherein CONSTANTINE, who alone of all that ever wielded the Roman power was the friend of God the Sovereign of all, has appeared to all mankind so clear an example of a godly life.

Charles T. Davis, *The Eagle, the Crescent, and the Cross.* New York: Appleton-Century-Crofts, 1967.

Document 2: The Nicene Creed

The Council of Nicaea, a meeting of Christian leaders called by Constantine in 324, established the mainstream Christian doctrine that both God and Jesus shared the same substance. Therefore, Jesus was himself divine. Heresies such as Arianism, which claimed that Jesus was human only, were condemned at Nicaea. Bishop Eusebius of Caesarea wrote to his congregation of the decision, quoting in full the Nicene Creed, which is still used widely today.

What was transacted concerning the faith of the Church at the Great Council assembled at Nicaea, you have probably learned, Beloved, from other sources, rumour being wont to precede the accurate account of what is doing. But lest in such reports the circumstances of the case have been misrepresented, we have been obliged to transmit to you, first, the formula of faith presented by ourselves; and next, the second, which they have published with additions to our words. Our own formulary, then, which was read in the presence of our most pious Emperor, and declared to be good and unexceptionable:—

As we have received from the Bishops who preceded us, and in our first catechizings, and when we received baptism, and as we have learned from the divine Scriptures, and as we constantly believed and taught as presbyter and bishop, so believing also at the time present, we report to you our faith, and it is this:—

"We believe in One God, Father Almighty, the Maker of all things visible and invisible. And in One Lord Jesus Christ, the Word of God, God from God, Light from Light, Life from Life, Only begotten Son, first-born of all creation, before all the ages begotten from the Father, by Whom also all things were made; Who for our salvation was incarnate, and lived among men, and suffered, and rose again the third day, and ascended to the Father, and will come again in glory to judge living and dead. And we believe also in One Holy Spirit":

Believing each of these to be and to exist, the Father truly Father, and the Son truly Son, and the Holy Spirit truly Holy Spirit, as also our Lord, sending forth His disciples for the preaching, said, *Go, teach all nations, baptizing them in the Name of the Father and of the Son and of the Holy Spirit.* Concerning whom we confidently affirm that so we hold, and so we think, and so we have held aforetime, and we maintain this faith unto the death, anathematizing every godless heresy. That this we have ever thought from our heart and soul, from the time we recollect ourselves, and now think and say in truth, before God Almighty and our Lord Jesus Christ do we witness, being able by proofs to show and to convince you that, in times past also, we constantly believed and preached thus.

Charles T. Davis, *The Eagle, the Crescent, and the Cross.* New York: Appleton-Century-Crofts, 1967.

Document 3: The Supremacy of the Bishop of Rome

Pope Leo I (440–461) was among the first to formally assert that the bishops of Rome were superior to all other bishops in the Empire. Their authority over Christians, he claimed, was descended from St. Peter, the first bishop of Rome. Consequently, only Roman bishops should be referred to as "papa," or pope.

Although, therefore, dearly beloved, we be found both weak and slothful in fulfilling the duties of our office, because, whatever devoted and vigorous action we desire to do, we are hindered by the frailty of our very condition; yet having the unceasing propitiation of the Almighty and perpetual Priest, who being like us and yet equal with the Father, brought down His Godhead even to things human, and raised His Manhood even to things Divine, we worthily and piously rejoice over His dispensation, whereby, though He has delegated the care of His sheep to many shepherds, yet He has not Himself abandoned the guardianship of His beloved flock. And from His overruling and eternal protection we have received the support of the Apostles' aid also, which assuredly does not cease from its operation: and the strength of the foundation, on which the whole superstructure of the Church is reared, is not weakened by the weight of the temple that rests upon it. For the solidity of that faith which was praised in the chief of the Apostles is perpetual: and as that remains which Peter believed in Christ, so that remains which Christ instituted in Peter. For when, as has been read in the Gospel lesson, the Lord had asked the disciples whom they believed Him to be amid the various opinions that were held, and the blessed Peter had replied, saying, "Thou art the Christ, the Son of the living GOD," the Lord said, "Blessed art thou, Simon Bar-Jona, because flesh and blood hath not revealed it to thee, but My Father, which is in heaven. And I say to thee, that thou art Peter, and upon this rock will I build My church, and the gates of Hades shall not prevail against it. And I will give unto thee the keys of the kingdom of heaven. And whatsoever thou shalt bind on earth, shall be bound in heaven; and whatsoever thou shalt loose on earth, shall be loosed also in heaven."

The dispensation of Truth therefore abides, and the blessed Peter persevering in the strength of the Rock, which he has received, has not abandoned the helm of the Church, which he undertook. For he was ordained before the rest in such a way that from his being called the Rock, from his being pronounced the Foundation, from his being constituted the Doorkeeper of the kingdom of heaven, from his being set as the Umpire to bind and to loose, whose judgments shall retain their validity in heaven, from all these mystical titles we might know the nature of his association with Christ. And still to-day he more fully and effectually performs what is entrusted to him, and carries out every part of his duty and charge in Him and with Him, through Whom he has been glorified. And so if anything is rightly done and rightly decreed by us, if anything is won from the mercy of GOD by our daily supplications, it is of his work and merits whose power lives and whose authority prevails in his See. For this, dearly-beloved, was gained by that confession, which, inspired in the Apostle's heart by GOD the Father, transcended all the uncertainty of human opinions, and was endued with the firmness of a rock, which no assaults could shake. For throughout the Church Peter daily says, "Thou art the Christ, the Son of the living GOD," and every tongue which confesses the Lord, accepts the instruction his voice conveys. This Faith conquers the devil, and breaks the bonds of his prisoners. It uproots us from this earth and plants us in heaven, and the gates of Hades cannot prevail against it. For with such solidity is it endued by GOD that the depravity of heretics cannot mar it nor the unbelief of the heathen overcome it.

Charles T. Davis, *The Eagle, the Crescent, and the Cross.* New York: Appleton-Century-Crofts, 1967.

Document 4: Monastic Discipline

Benedict's Rule, written between 520 and 530, sought to describe the duties and discipline necessary in communities of monks. Not only should they pray and study, they should engage in labor and obey the authority of their abbots.

48. *Concerning the daily manual labor.* Idleness is the enemy of the soul. And therefore, at fixed times, the brothers ought to be occupied in manual labor; and again, at fixed times, in sacred reading. Therefore we believe that both seasons ought to be arranged after this manner,—so that, from Easter until the Calends of October, going out early, from the first until the fourth hour they shall do what labor may be necessary. From the fourth hour until about the sixth, they shall be free for reading. After the meal of the sixth hour, rising from the table, they shall rest in their beds with all silence; or, perchance, he that wishes to read may read to himself in such a way as not to disturb another. And the *nona* [the second meal] shall be gone through with more moderately about the mid-

dle of the eighth hour; and again they shall work at what is to be done until Vespers. But, if the emergency or poverty of the place demands that they be occupied in picking fruits, they shall not be grieved; for they are truly monks if they live by the labors of their hands, as did also our fathers and the apostles. Let all things be done with moderation, however, on account of the faint-hearted.

In days of Lent they shall all receive separate books from the library, which they shall read entirely through in order. These books are to be given out on the first day of Lent. Above all there shall be appointed without fail one or two elders, who shall go round the monastery at the hours in which the brothers are engaged in reading, and see to it that no troublesome brother be found who is given to idleness and trifling, and is not intent on his reading, being not only of no use to himself, but also stirring up others. If such a one (may it not happen) be found, he shall be reproved once and a second time. If he do not amend, he shall be subject under the Rule to such punishment that the others may have fear. Nor shall brother join brother at unsuitable hours. Moreover, on Sunday all shall engage in reading, excepting those who are assigned to various duties. But if any one be so negligent and lazy that he will not or can not read, some task shall be imposed upon him which he can do, so that he be not idle. On feeble or delicate brothers such a task or art is to be imposed, that they shall neither be idle nor so oppressed by the violence of labor as to be driven to take flight. Their weakness is to be taken into consideration by the abbot.

Frederick Austin Ogg, *A Source Book of Medieval History*. New York: American Book Company, 1908.

Document 5: The Huns

The Romans found the Huns, who invaded Europe from Central Asia in waves in the fourth and fifth centuries, to be very different from them. The historian Ammianus Marcellinus noted their battlefield tactics and bravery as well as their nomadic habits.

When a discussion arises upon any matter of importance they come on horseback to the place of meeting. No kingly sternness overawes their deliberations, but being, on the whole, well-contented with the disorderly guidance of their chiefs, they do not scruple to interrupt the debates with anything that comes into their heads. When attacked, they will sometimes engage in regular battle. Then, going into the fight in order of columns, they fill the air with varied and discordant cries. More often, however, they fight in no regular order of battle, but being extremely swift and sudden in their movements, they disperse, and then rapidly come together again in loose array, spread havoc over vast plains and, flying over the rampart, pillage the camp of their enemy almost before he has become aware of their approach. It must be granted that they are the nimblest of warriors. The missile weapons which they use at a distance are pointed with sharpened bones admirably fastened to the shaft. When in close combat they fight without regard to their own safety, and while the enemy is intent upon parrying the thrusts of their swords they throw a net over him and so entangle his limbs that he loses all power of walking or riding.

Not one among them cultivates the ground, or ever touches a plow-handle. All wander abroad without fixed abodes, without home, or law, or settled customs, like perpetual fugitives, with their wagons for their only habitations. If you ask them, not one can tell you what is his place of origin. They are ruthless truce-breakers, fickle, always ready to be swayed by the first breath of a new desire, abandoning themselves without restraint to the most ungovernable rage.

Frederick Austin Ogg, *A Source Book of Medieval History*. New York: American Book Company, 1908.

Document 6: Clovis, King of the Franks, Converts to Christianity

The Franks, following the example of Clovis, were the first Germanic tribe to convert to Roman Catholic Christianity. The Chronicler Gregory of Tours remembered that it was events in battle that finally urged Clovis to follow the guidance of his wife, already a Christian, and adopt the new faith.

The queen did not cease urging the king to acknowledge the true God and forsake idols, but all her efforts failed until at length a war broke out with the Alemanni. Then of necessity he was compelled to confess what hitherto he had wilfully denied. It happened that the two armies were in battle and there was great slaughter. The army of Clovis seemed about to be cut in pieces. Then the king raised his hands fervently toward the heavens and, breaking into tears, cried: "Jesus Christ, who Clotilde declares to be the son of the living God, who it is said givest help to the oppressed and victory to those who put their trust in thee, I invoke thy marvellous help. If thou wilt give me victory over my enemies and I prove that power which thy followers say they have proved concerning thee, I will believe in thee and will be baptized in thy name; for I have called upon my own gods and it is clear that they have neglected to give me aid. Therefore I am convinced that they have no power, for they do not help those who serve them. I now call upon thee, and I wish to believe in thee, especially that I may escape from my enemies." When he had offered this prayer the Alemanni turned their backs and began to flee. And when they learned that their king had been slain, they submitted at once to Clovis, saying, "Let no more of our people perish, for we now belong to you." When he had stopped the battle and praised his soldiers for their good work, Clovis returned in peace to his kingdom and told the queen how he had won the victory by calling on the name of Christ. These events took place in the fifteenth year of his reign.

Frederick Austin Ogg, *A Source Book of Medieval History.* New York: American Book Company, 1908.

Document 7: Germanic Laws

Early Germanic society could be extremely violent. Punishment, however, might take the form of "wergeld," which was a cash payment thought to be equal to the crime. The laws of Ethelbert, king of Kent, who was one of the Anglo-Saxon rulers of Britain, show how precise wergeld could be.

27] IF a freeman breaks the fence round [another man's] enclosure, he shall pay 6 shillings compensation.

28] If any property be seized therein, the man shall pay a three fold compensation.

29] If a freeman makes his way into a fenced enclosure, he shall pay 4 shillings compensation.

30] If one man slays another, he shall pay the wergeld with his own money and property (i.e. livestock or other goods) which whatever its nature must be free from blemish [or damage].

31] If [one] freeman lies with the wife of [another] freeman, he shall pay [the husband] his [or her] wergeld, and procure a second wife with his own money, and bring her to the other man's home.

32] If anyone damages the enclosure of a dwelling, he shall pay according to its value.

33] For seizing a man by the hair, 50 sceattas shall be paid as compensation.

34] If a bone is laid bare, 3 shillings shall be paid as compensation.

35] If a bone is damaged, 4 shillings shall be paid as compensation.

36] If the outer covering of the skull is broken, 10 shillings shall be paid as compensation.

37] If both are broken, 20 shillings shall be paid as compensation.

38] If a shoulder is disabled, 30 shillings shall be paid as compensation.

39] If the hearing of either ear is destroyed, 25 shillings shall be paid as compensation.

40] If an ear is struck off, 12 shillings shall be paid as compensation.

41] If an ear is pierced, 3 shillings shall be paid as compensation.

42] If an ear is lacerated, 6 shillings shall be paid as compensation.

43] If an eye is knocked out, 50 shillings shall be paid as compensation.

44] If the mouth or an eye is disfigured, 12 shillings shall be paid as compensation.

45] If the nose is pierced, 9 shillings shall be paid as compensation.

46] If it is one cheek, 3 shillings shall be paid as compensation.

47] If both are pierced, 6 shillings shall be paid as compensation.

48] If the nose is lacerated otherwise [than by piercing], 6 shillings shall be paid as compensation, for each laceration.

49] If it is pierced, 6 shillings shall be paid as compensation.

50] He who smashes a chin bone, shall pay for it with 20 shillings.

51] For each of the 4 front teeth, 6 shillings [shall be paid as compensation]; for each of the teeth which stand next to these, 4 shillings [shall be paid as compensation]; then for each tooth which stands next to them, 3 shillings [shall be paid as compensation]; and beyond that 1 shilling [shall be paid as compensation] for each tooth.

52] If the power of speech is injured, 12 shillings [shall be paid as compensation].

§1. If a collar bone is injured, 6 shillings shall be paid as compensation.

53] He who pierces an arm shall pay 6 shillings compensation.

§1. If an arm is broken, 6 shillings shall be paid as compensation.

54] If a thumb is struck off, 20 shillings [shall be paid as compensation].

§1. If a thumb nail is knocked off, 3 shillings shall be paid as compensation.

§2. If a man strikes off a forefinger, he shall pay 9 shillings compensation.

§3. If a man strikes off a middle finger, he shall pay 4 shillings compensation.

§4. If a man strikes off a 'ring finger,' he shall pay 6 shillings compensation.

§5. If a man strikes off a little finger, he shall pay 11 shillings compensation.

55] For the nails of each [of the above-mentioned fingers], 1 shilling [shall be paid as compensation].

56] For the slightest disfigurement, 3 shillings, and for a greater 6 shillings [shall be paid as compensation].

Robert Brentano, ed., *The Early Middle Ages: 500–1000*, New York: The Free Press, 1964.

Document 8: Justinian's Code of Law

The Byzantine emperor Justinian wanted to collect Roman law and make it understandable and accessible. Among his collections was the In-stitutes, *a guide for younger scholars.*

Justice is the constant and perpetual desire to give to each one that to which he is entitled.

Jurisprudence is the knowledge of matters divine and human, and the comprehension of what is just and what is unjust.

These divisions being generally understood, and We being about to explain the laws of the Roman people, it appears that this may be most conveniently done if separate subjects are at first treated in a clear and simple manner, and afterwards with greater care and exactness; for if We, at once, in the beginning, load the still uncultivated and inexperienced mind of the student with a multitude and variety of details, We shall bring about one of two things; that is, We shall either cause him to abandon his studies, or, by means of excessive labor—and also with that distrust which very frequently discourages young men—conduct him to that point to which, if led by an easier route, he might have been brought more speedily without much exertion and without misgiving.

The following are the precepts of the Law: to live honestly, not to injure another, and to give to each one that which belongs to him.

There are two branches of this study, namely: public and private. Public Law is that which concerns the administration of the Roman government; Private Law relates to the interests of individuals. Thus Private Law is said to be threefold in its nature, for it is composed of precepts of Natural Law, of those of the Law of Nations, and of those of the Civil Law.

Charles T. Davis, *The Eagle, the Crescent, and the Cross*. New York: Appleton-Century-Crofts, 1967.

Document 9: The Use of Icons in Christianity

In the seventh and eighth centuries the Byzantine Church was torn by controversy over whether holy images, or icons, should be used in Christ-

ian ritual. The religious thinker St. John of Damascus claimed that icons enhanced Christianity.

Again, an image is expressive of something in the future, mystically shadowing forth what is to happen. For instance, the ark represents the image of Our Lady, Mother of God, so does the staff and the earthen jar. The serpent brings before us Him who vanquished on the Cross the bite of the original serpent; the sea, water, and the cloud the grace of baptism.

Again, things which have taken place are expressed by images for the remembrance either of a wonder, or an honour, or dishonour, or good or evil, to help those who look upon it in after times that we may avoid evils and imitate goodness. It is of two kinds, the written image in books, as when God had the law inscribed on tablets, and when He enjoined that the lives of holy men should be recorded and sensible memorials be preserved in remembrance as, for instance, the earthen jar and the staff in the ark. So now we preserve in writing the images and the good deeds of the past. Either, therefore, take away images altogether and be out of harmony with God who made these regulations, or receive them with the language and in the manner which befits them.

Charles T. Davis, *The Eagle, the Crescent, and the Cross.* New York: Appleton-Century-Crofts, 1967.

Document 10: Celebrating Icons

Worship in the Byzantine Empire could be very elaborate, especially at the Church of Hagia Sophia, the greatest church in Constantinople. The religious leader of the church in the mid-ninth century, Patriarch Photius, conducted a rich ceremony celebrating the unveiling of an icon of the Virgin Mary and the Christ Child.

But the cause of the celebration, whereby today's feast is conspicuously adorned, is, as we have already said, the following: splendid piety erecting trophies against belief hostile to Christ; impiety lying low, stripped of her very last hopes; and the ungodly ideas of those half-barbarous and bastard clans which had crept into the Roman government (who were an insult and a disgrace to the emperors) being exposed to everyone as an object of hatred and aversion. Yea, and as for us, beloved pair of pious Emperors, shining forth from the purple, connected with the dearest names of father and son, and not allowing the name to belie the relationship, but striving to set in all other aspects also an example of superhuman love, whose preoccupation is Orthodoxy rather than pride in the imperial diadem,—it is in these things that the deed which is before our eyes instigates us to take pride. With such a welcome does the representation of the Virgin's form cheer us, inviting us to draw not from a bowl of wine, but from a fair spectacle, by which the rational part of our soul, being watered through our bodily eyes, and given eyesight in its growth towards the divine love of Orthodoxy, puts forth in the way of fruit the most exact vision of truth. Thus, even in her images does the Virgin's grace delight, comfort and strengthen us! A virgin mother carrying in her pure arms, for the common salvation of our kind, the common Creator reclining as an infant—that great and ineffable mystery of the Dispensation! A virgin mother, with a virgin's and a mother's gaze, dividing in indivisible form her temperament between both capacities, yet belittling neither by its incompleteness. With such exactitude has the art of painting, which is a reflection of inspiration from above, set up a lifelike imitation. For, as it were, she fondly turns her eyes on her begotten Child in the affection of her heart, yet assumes the expression of a detached and imperturbable mood at the passionless and wondrous nature of her offspring, and composes her gaze accordingly. You might think her not incapable of speaking, even if one were to ask her, "How didst thou give birth and remainest a virgin?" To such an extent have the lips been made flesh by the colours, that they appear merely to be pressed together and stilled as in the mysteries, yet their silence is not at all inert neither is the fairness of her form derivatory, but rather is it the real archetype.

Robert Brentano, ed., *The Early Middle Ages: 500–1000.* New York: The Free Press, 1964.

Document 11: Islamic Conquests in the Near East

The Arab chronicler al-Baladhuri noted that, despite a huge army raised by the Byzantine emperor Heraclius, the Muslims were still victorious at the Battle of Yarmuk in 636.

Heraclius gathered large bodies of Greeks, Syrians, Mesopotamians and Armenians numbering about 200,000. This army he put under the command of one of his choice men and sent as a vanguard Jabalah ibn-al-Aiham al-Ghassani at the head of the "naturalized" Arabs of Syria of the tribes of Lakhm, Judham and others, resolving to fight the Moslems so that he might either win or withdraw to the land of the Greeks and live in Constantinople. The Moslems gathered together and the Greek army marched against them. The battle they fought at al-Yarmuk was of the fiercest and bloodiest kind. Al-Yarmuk [Hieromax] is a river. In this battle

24,000 Moslems took part. The Greeks and their followers in this battle tied themselves to each other by chains, so that no one might set his hope on flight. By Allah's help, some 70,000 of them were put to death, and their remnants took to flight, reaching as far as Palestine, Antioch, Aleppo, Mesopotamia and Armenia. In the battle of al-Yarmuk certain Moslem women took part and fought violently. Among them was Hind, daughter of 'Utbah and mother of Mu'awiyah ibn-abi-Sufyan, who repeatedly exclaimed, "Cut the arms of these 'uncircumcised' with your swords!" Her husband abu-Sufvan had come to Syria as a volunteer desiring to see his sons, and so he brought his wife with him. He then returned to al-Madinah where he died, year 31, at the age of 88. Others say he died in Syria. When the news of his death was carried to his daughter, umm-Habibah, she waited until the third day on which she ordered some yellow paint and covered with it her arms and face saying, "I would not have done that, had I not heard the Prophet say, 'A woman should not be in mourning for more than three days over anyone except her husband.'" It is stated that she did likewise when she received the news of her brother Yazid's death. But Allah knows best.

Charles T. Davis, *The Eagle, the Crescent, and the Cross.* New York: Appleton-Century-Crofts, 1967.

Document 12: A Forgery: The Donation of Constantine

In the eighth century, the papacy struggled to maintain its independence in the face of the Lombards and the Franks. One tool they used was the Donation of Constantine, a document in which Constantine claimed that the popes, not kings, were the true descendants of the Roman emperors. In the 1400s, however, the document was proven to be false.

And we decree, as to those most reverend men, the clergy who serve, in different orders, that same holy Roman church, that they shall have the same advantage, distinction, power and excellence by the glory of which our most illustrious senate is adorned; that is, that they shall be made patricians and consuls,—we commanding that they shall also be decorated with the other imperial dignities. And even as the imperial soldiery, so, we decree, shall the clergy of the holy Roman church be adorned. And even as the imperial power is adorned by different offices—by the distinction, that is, of chamberlains, and door keepers, and all the guards,—so we wish the holy Roman church to be adorned. And, in order that the pontifical glory may shine forth more fully, we decree this also:

that the clergy of this same holy Roman church may use saddle cloths of linen of the whitest colour; namely that their horses may be adorned and so be ridden, and that, as our senate uses shoes with goats' hair, so they may be distinguished by gleaming linen; in order that, as the celestial beings, so the terrestrial may be adorned to the glory of God. Above all things moreover, we give permission to that same most holy one our father Sylvester, bishop of the city of Rome and pope, and to all the most blessed pontiffs who shall come after him and succeed him in all future times—for the honour and glory of Jesus Christ our Lord,—to receive into that great catholic and apostolic church of God, even into the number of the monastic clergy, any one from our senate, who, in free choice, of his own accord, may wish to become a cleric; no one at all presuming thereby to act in a haughty manner.

We also decreed this, that this same venerable one our father Sylvester, the supreme pontiff, and all the pontiffs his successors, might use and bear upon their heads—to the praise of God and for the honour of St. Peter—the diadem; that is, the crown which we have granted him from our own head, of purest gold and precious gems. But he, the most holy pope, did not at all allow that crown of gold to be used over the clerical crown which he wears to the glory of St. Peter; but we placed upon his most holy head, with our own hands, a tiara of gleaming splendour representing the glorious resurrection of our Lord. And, holding the bridle of his horse, out of reverence for St. Peter we performed for him the duty of groom; decreeing that all the pontiffs his successors, and they alone, may use that tiara in processions.

In imitation of our own power, in order that for that cause the supreme pontificate may not deteriorate, but may rather be adorned with power and glory even more than is the dignity of an earthly rule: behold we—giving over to the oft-mentioned most blessed pontiff, our father Sylvester the universal pope, as well our palace, as has been said, as also the city of Rome and all the provinces, districts and cities of Italy or of the western regions; and relinquishing them, by our inviolable gift, to the power and sway of himself or the pontiffs his successors—do decree, by this our godlike charter and imperial constitution, that it shall be (so) arranged; and do concede that they (the palaces, provinces etc.) shall lawfully remain with the holy Roman church.

Charles T. Davis, *The Eagle, the Crescent, and the Cross*. New York: Appleton-Century-Crofts, 1967.

Document 13: A Pope Asks for Help

In the 730s, Pope Gregory was beleaguered by the Lombards, a Germanic tribe which controlled most of Italy. He asked for military assistance and support from Charles Martel, the military leader of the Franks, promising God's favor in return. Since he belonged to the Carolingian rather than the Merovingian family, and could therefore not be king, Gregory referred to Charles as "Karl, sub-king."

Pope Gregory to his most excellent son, Karl, sub-king.

In our great affliction we have thought it necessary to write to you a second time, believing that you are a loving son of St. Peter, the prince of apostles, and of ourselves, and that out of reverence for him you would obey our commands to defend the church of God and his chosen people. We can now no longer endure the persecution of the Lombards, for they have taken from St. Peter all his possessions, even those which were given him by you and your fathers. These Lombards hate and oppress us because we sought protection from you; for the same reason also the church of St. Peter is despoiled and desolated by them. But we have intrusted a more complete account of all our woes to your faithful subject, our present messenger, and he will relate them to you. You, oh son, will receive favor from the same prince of apostles here and in the future life in the presence of God, according as you render speedy aid to his church and to us, that all peoples may recognize the faith and love and singleness of purpose which you display in defending St. Peter and us and his chosen people. For by doing this you will attain lasting fame on earth and eternal life in heaven.

Robert Brentano, ed., *The Early Middle Ages: 500–1000*. New York: The Free Press, 1964.

Document 14: Pepin III Accepts the Frankish Kingship

Unlike his father Charles Martel, Pepin III was willing to ally himself with the pope and be named king of the Franks along with his Carolingian successors. A chronicler noted how Pope Zacharias formally invested Pepin III with the kingship and sent the final Merovingian, Childeric, off in disgrace.

In the year 750 of the Lord's incarnation Pepin sent ambassadors to Rome to Pope Zacharias, to inquire concerning the kings of the Franks who, though they were of the royal line and were called kings, had no power in the kingdom, except that charters and privileges were drawn up in their names. They had absolutely no kingly authority, but did whatever the Major Domus of the Franks desired. But on the first day of March in the Campus Martius, according to ancient custom, gifts were offered to these kings by the people, and the king himself sat in the royal seat with the army standing round him and the Major Domus in his presence, and he commanded on that day whatever was decreed by the Franks; but on all other days thenceforward he remained quietly at home. Pope Zacharias, therefore, in the exercise of his apostolic authority, replied to their inquiry that it seemed to him better and more expedient that the man who held power in the kingdom should be called king and be king, rather than he who falsely bore that name. Therefore the aforesaid pope commanded the king and people of the Franks that Pepin, who was exercising royal power, should be called king, and should be established on the throne. This was therefore done by the anointing of the holy archbishop Boniface in the city of Soissons. Pepin was proclaimed king, and Childeric, who was falsely called king, was shaved and sent into a monastery.

Frederick Austin Ogg, *A Source Book of Medieval History*. New York: American Book Company, 1908.

Document 15: A Literary Commemoration of Charlemagne

One of the greatest works of early medieval literature is the Song of Roland, *which tells the story of, among other things, Charlemagne's success in defeating the Islamic invaders of France at the Battle of Roncesvals in 778. This passage also notes Charlemagne's status both in the eyes of his soldiers and in the eyes of God.*

For Charlemagne God worked a miracle,
because the sun is standing motionless.
The pagans flee, the Franks pursue them hard,
and overtake them at Val-Tenebrus.
They fight them on the run toward Saragossa;
with mighty blows they kill them as they go;
they cut them off from the main roads and the lanes.
The river Ebro lies in front of them,
a deep, swift-running, terrifying stream;
there's not a barge or boat or dromond there.
The pagans call on Termagant, their god,
and then leap in, but nothing will protect them.
The men in armor are the heaviest,
and numbers of them plummet to the bottom;
the other men go floating off downstream.
The best equipped thus get their fill to drink;

they all are drowned in dreadful agony.
The Frenchmen cry out: "You were luckless, Roland!"

As soon as Charles sees all the pagans dead
(some killed, a greater number of them drowned)
and rich spoils taken off them by his knights,
the noble king then climbs down to his feet,
prostrates himself, and offers thanks to God.
When he gets up again, the sun has set.
"It's time to pitch camp," says the emperor.
"It's too late to go back to Roncesvals.
Our horses are fatigued and ridden down;
unsaddle them and then unbridle them
and turn them out to cool off in this field."
The Franks reply: "Sire, you have spoken well."

The emperor has picked a place to camp.
The French dismount upon the open land
and pull the saddles off their destriers
and take the gold-trimmed bridles from their heads,
then turn them out to graze the thick green grass;
there's nothing else that they can do for them.
The tiredest go to sleep right on the ground:
that night they post no sentinels at all.

The emperor has lain down in a meadow.
The brave lord sets his great lance at his head—
tonight he does not wish to be unarmed—
keeps on his shiny, saffron-yellow hauberk,
and his jeweled golden helmet, still laced up,
and at his waist Joyeuse, which has no peer:
its brilliance alters thirty times a day.
We've heard a great deal spoken of the lance
with which Our Lord was wounded on the cross;
that lance's head is owned by Charles, thank God;
he had its tip inletted in the pommel.
Because of this distinction and this grace,
the name "Joyeuse" was given to the sword.
The Frankish lords will not forget this fact:
they take from it their battle cry, "Monjoy."
Because of this, no race can stand against them.

The Song of Roland, trans. Robert Harrison. New York: Mentor/Penguin, 1970.

Document 16: Charlemagne is Crowned Holy Roman Emperor

Anonymous chroniclers recorded how, on Christmas Day, 800, Charlemagne was formally invested with the title of Holy Roman Emperor by Pope Leo III. Both emperor and pope saw the coronation as a revival of the Roman Empire in western Europe.

And because the name of emperor had now ceased among the Greeks, and their empire was possessed by a woman, it seemed both to Leo the pope himself, and to all the holy fathers who were present in the self-same council, as well as to the rest of the Christian people, that they ought to take to be emperor Charles, king of the Franks, who held Rome herself, where the Caesars had always been wont to sit, and all the other regions which he ruled through Italy and Gaul and Germany; and inasmuch as God had given all these lands into his hand, it seemed right that with the help of God, and at the prayer of the whole Christian people, he should have the name of emperor also. [The Pope's] petition King Charles willed not to refuse, but submitting himself with all humility to God, and at the prayer of the priests, and of the whole Christian people, on the day of the nativity of our Lord Jesus Christ, he took on himself the name of emperor, being consecrated by the Pope Leo. . . . For this also was done by the will of God . . . that the heathen might not mock the Christians if the name of emperor should have ceased among them.

After these things, on the day of the birth of our Lord Jesus Christ, when all the people were assembled in the Church of the blessed St. Peter, the venerable and gracious Pope with his own hands crowned him [Charlemagne] with an exceedingly precious crown. Then all the faithful Romans, beholding the choice of such a friend and defender of the holy Roman Church, and of the pontiff, did by the will of God and of the blessed Peter, the key-bearer of the heavenly kingdom, cry with a loud voice, "To Charles, the most pious Augustus, crowned of God, the great and peace-giving Emperor, be life and victory." While he, before the altar of the church was calling upon many of the saints, it was proclaimed three times, and by the common voice of all he was chosen to be emperor of the Romans. Then the most holy high priest and pontiff anointed Charles with holy oil, and also his most excellent son to be king, upon the very day of the birth of our Lord Jesus Christ.

Frederick Austin Ogg, *A Source Book of Medieval History*. New York: American Book Company, 1908.

Document 17: Study Encouraged

Although he was himself illiterate, Charlemagne had a strong faith in the expansion of literacy and education. He decreed that study of the Holy Scriptures made one more pleasing to God.

We, together with our faithful, have considered it to be useful that the bishoprics and monasteries entrusted by the favor of Christ to our control, in addition to the order of monastic life and the intercourse of holy religion, in the culture of letters also ought to be zealous in teaching those who by the gift of God are able to learn, according to the capacity of each individual, so that just as the observance of the rule imparts order and grace to honesty of morals, so also zeal in teaching and learning may do the same for sentences, so that those who desire to please God by living rightly should not neglect to please him also by speaking correctly. For it is written: "Either from thy words thou shalt be justified or from thy words thou shalt be condemned." For although correct conduct may be better than knowledge, nevertheless knowledge precedes conduct. Therefore, each one ought to study what he desires to accomplish, so that so much the more fully the mind may know what ought to be done, as the tongue hastens in the praises of omnipotent God without the hindrances of errors. For since errors should be shunned by all men, so much the more ought they to be avoided as far as possible by those who are chosen for this very purpose alone, so that they ought to be the especial servants of truth. For when in the years just passed letters were often written to us from several monasteries in which it was stated that the brethren who dwelt there offered up in our behalf sacred and pious prayers, we have recognized in most of these letters both correct thoughts and uncouth expressions; because what pious devotion dictated faithfully to the mind, the tongue, uneducated on account of the neglect of study, was not able to express in the letter without error. Whence it happened that we began to fear lest perchance, as the skill in writing was less, so also the wisdom for understanding the Holy Scriptures might be much less than it rightly ought to be. And we all know well that, although errors of speech are dangerous, far more dangerous are errors of the understanding. Therefore, we exhort you not only not to neglect the study of letters, but also with most humble mind, pleasing to God, to study earnestly in order that you may be able more easily and more correctly to penetrate the mysteries of the divine Scriptures. Since, moreover, images, tropes and similar figures are found in the sacred pages, no one doubts that each one in reading these will understand the spiritual sense more quickly if previously he shall have been fully instructed in the mastery of letters. Such men truly are to be chosen for this work as have both the will and the ability to learn and a desire to instruct others. And may this be done with a zeal as great as the earnestness with which we command it. For we desire you to be, as it is fitting that soldiers of the church should be, devout in mind, learned in discourse, chaste in conduct and eloquent in speech, so that whosoever shall seek to see you out of reverence for God, or on account of your reputation for holy conduct, just as he is edified by your appearance, may also be instructed by your wisdom, which he has learned from your reading or singing, and may go away joyfully giving thanks to omnipotent God.

Charles T. Davis, *The Eagle, the Crescent, and the Cross.* New York: Appleton-Century-Crofts, 1967.

Document 18: Viking Invasions

From the late eighth century to the eleventh century, Viking raiders from Scandinavia threatened the more settled parts of Europe. Medieval historians noted how they attacked and plundered cities and monasteries, but could also be defeated or bought off.

845. The Northmen with a hundred ships entered the Seine on the twentieth of March and, after ravaging first one bank and then the other, came without meeting any resistance to Paris. Charles resolved to hold out against them; but seeing the impossibility of gaining a victory, he made with them a certain agreement and by a gift of 7,000 livres he bought them off from advancing farther and persuaded them to return.

Euric, king of the Northmen, advanced, with six hundred vessels, along the course of the River Elbe to attack Louis of Germany. The Saxons prepared to meet him, gave battle, and with the aid of our Lord Jesus Christ won the victory.

The Northmen returned [from Paris] down the Seine and coming to the ocean pillaged, destroyed, and burned all the regions along the coast.

846. The Danish pirates landed in Frisia. They were able to force from the people whatever contributions they wished and, being victors in battle, they remained masters of almost the entire province.

847. The Northmen made their appearance in the part of Gaul inhabited by the Britons and won three victories. Noménoé, al-

though defeated, at length succeeded in buying them off with presents and getting them out of his country.

853–854. The Danish pirates, making their way into the country eastward from the city of Nantes, arrived without opposition, November eighth, before Tours. This they burned, together with the church of St. Martin and the neighboring places. But that incursion had been foreseen with certainty and the body of St. Martin had been removed to Cormery, a monastery of that church, and from there to the city of Orleans. The pirates went on to the chateâu of Blois and burned it, proposing then to proceed to Orleans and destroy that city in the same fashion. But Agius, bishop of Orleans, and Burchard, bishop of Chartres, had gathered soldiers and ships to meet them; so they abandoned their design and returned to the lower Loire, though the following year [855] they ascended it anew to the city of Angers.

Frederick Austin Ogg, *A Source Book of Medieval History*. New York: American Book Company, 1908.

Document 19: A Feudal Lord's Household

This precise record of the goods of one of Charlemagne's estates helps indicate the mode of life of even the most powerful Europeans. Throughout the Early Middle Ages, Europe remained overwhelmingly rural, and life was spartan.

We found in the domain estate of Asnapium a royal house built of stone in the best manner, 3 rooms; the whole house surrounded with balconies, with 11 apartments for women; beneath 1 cellar; 2 porticoes; 17 other houses built of wood within the court-yard with as many rooms and other appurtenances, well built; 1 stable, 1 kitchen, 1 mill, 1 granary, 3 barns.

The yard surrounded carefully with a hedge and stone gateway and above a balcony from which to make distributions. An inner yard, likewise enclosed within a hedge, arranged in a suitable manner planted with various kinds of trees.

Vestments: coverings for 1 bed, 1 table cloth, 1 towel.

Utensils: 2 brass kettles, 2 drinking cups, 2 brass cauldrons, 1 iron one, 1 frying-pan, 1 gramalmin, 1 pair of andirons, 1 lamp, 2 hatchets, 1 chisel, 2 augers, 1 axe, 1 knife, 1 large plane, 1 plane, 2 scythes, 2 sickles, 2 spades tipped with iron. Enough wooden utensils for use.

Farm produce: old spelt from last year, 90 baskets which can be made into 450 weight of flour; 100 measures of barley. From the present year, 110 baskets of spelt, planted 60 baskets from the same, the rest we found; 100 measures of wheat, 60 sown, the rest we found; 98 measures of rye all sown; 1800 measures of barley, 1100 sown, the rest we found; 430 measures of oats, 1 measure of beans, 12 measures of peas. At the 5 mills, 800 measures, small measures. At the 4 breweries, 650 measures, small measures, 240 given to the prebendaries, the rest we found. At the 2 bridges, 60 measures of salt and 2 shillings. At the 4 gardens, 11 shillings. Honey, 3 measures; about 1 measure of butter; lard, from last year 10 sides, new sides 200 with fragments and fats, cheese from the present year 43 weights.

Of cattle: 51 head of larger cattle, 5 three-year-olds, 7 two-year-olds, 7 yearlings; 10 two-year-old colts, 8 yearlings, 3 stallions; 16 cows; 2 asses; 50 cows with calves, 20 young bullocks, 38 yearling calves, 3 bulls, 260 hogs, 100 pigs, 5 boars, 150 sheep with lambs, 200 yearling lambs, 120 rams, 30 goats with kids, 30 yearling kids, 2 male goats, 30 geese, 80 chickens, 22 peacocks.

Also concerning the dependencies which pertain to the above mansion. In the villa of Grisio we found domain buildings, where there are 3 barns and a yard surrounded by a hedge. There is there 1 garden with trees, 10 geese, 8 ducks, 30 chickens.

In another villa. We found domain buildings and a yard surrounded by a hedge and within 3 barns, 1 arpent of vines, 1 garden with trees, 15 geese, 20 chickens.

In a third villa, domain buildings. It has 2 barns, 1 granary, 1 garden, 1 yard well enclosed by a hedge.

We found all the dry and liquid measures just as in the palace. We did not find any goldsmiths, silversmiths, blacksmiths, huntsmen or persons engaged in other services.

The garden herbs which we found were lily, putchuck, mint, parsley, rue, celery, *libesticum*, sage, savory, juniper, leeks, garlic, tansy, wild mint, coriander, scullions, onions, cabbage, kohl-rabi, betony. Trees: pears, apples, medlars, peaches, filberts, walnuts, mulberries, quinces.

Robert Brentano, ed., *The Early Middle Ages: 500–1000*. New York: The Free Press, 1964.

Document 20: Feudal Obligations

Anonymous medieval chroniclers recorded how the establishment of feudal ties required the performance of homage, or ceremonies of subservience. In addition, they noted that the oath of fealty was binding on both lord and vassal.

And when a free tenant shall swear fealty to his lord, let him place his right hand on the book and speak thus: "Hear thou this, my lord, that I will be faithful and loyal to you and will keep my pledges to you for the lands which I claim to hold of you, and that I will loyally perform for you the services specified, so help me God and the saints." Then he shall kiss the book; but he shall not kneel when he swears fealty, nor take so humble a posture as is required in homage. . . .

If any one would hold from a lord in fee, he ought to seek his lord within forty days. And if he does not do it within forty days, the lord may and ought to seize his fief for default of homage, and the things which are found there he should seize without compensation; and yet the vassal should be obliged to pay to his lord the redemption. When any one wishes to enter into the fealty of a lord, he ought to seek him, as we have said above, and should speak as follows: "Sir, I request you, as my lord, to put me in your fealty and in your homage for such and such a thing situated in your fief, which I have bought." And he ought to say from what man, and this one ought to be present and in the fealty of the lord; and whether it is by purchase or by escheat, or by inheritance he ought to explain; and with his hands joined, to speak as follows: "Sir, I become your man and promise to you fealty for the future as my lord, towards all men who may live or die, rendering to you such service as the fief requires, making to you your relief as you are the lord." And he ought to say whether for guardianship, or as an escheat, or as an inheritance, or as a purchase.

The lord should immediately reply to him: "And I receive you and take you as my man, and give you this kiss as a sign of faith, saving my right and that of others," according to the usage of the various districts.

Frederick Austin Ogg, *A Source Book of Medieval History*. New York: American Book Company, 1908.

Chronology

306
Constantine becomes Roman emperor.

324
The Greek city of Byzantium is renamed Constantinople and becomes the new capital of the Roman Empire.

325
The Council of Nicaea condemns the Arian heresy.

337
Constantine is baptised into Christianity; he is the first Christian emperor.

378
At the Battle of Adrianople, the Roman army is betrayed and attacked by its Visigothic allies. The emperor, Valens, is killed.

380
The Roman emperor Theodosius proclaims Christianity to be the official religion of the Roman Empire.

410
Alaric the Visogoth and his army sack Rome.

413–426
In the wake of the Roman Empire being overrun by invaders, St. Augustine writes *City of God*.

440–461
Leo I, who believes strongly that the bishop of Rome should be the head of all bishops, is the bishop of Rome. He is called "papa" or pope by supporters.

451
At the Council of Chalcedon, Christian leaders condemn the Monophysite heresy.

451–453
Attila the Hun and his armies invade the Roman Empire.

455
The Germanic Vandals sack Rome.

476

The final Western Roman emperor, Romulus Augustulus, is deposed by the Germanic warlord, Odovacer. The event marks the end of the Roman Empire in the west, as Odovacer is recognized as the leader in the west by Zeno, the Byzantine emperor.

493–526

Theodoric, king of the Ostrogoths, establishes a strong kingdom in Italy and threatens the Byzantine Empire.

496

Clovis, king of the Franks, converts to Roman Catholic Christianity along with much of his army. The Franks are the first of the Germanic tribes to convert to Roman Catholicism.

ca. 500

Anglo-Saxon invaders confront a Celtic army led by a warrior known as Arthur in Britain.

529

St. Benedict establishes his monastery at Monte Cassino in Italy. It operates according to Benedict's *Rule*, written between 520 and 530.

533

The Byzantine emperor Justinian begins to assemble his collection of Roman law.

535–552

Much of Italy is reconquered by the Byzantines.

537

Construction of the Church of Hagia Sophia in Constantinople is completed.

568

The Germanic Lombards invade Italy.

590–604

Gregory the First, or Gregory the Great, is pope. He helps establish the primacy of the papacy by turning it into an administrative as well as religious institution.

622

Muhammad forms the first Islamic community at Medina in Arabia.

636

The Byzantine Empire suffers a major defeat at the hands of Arab Muslims at the Battle of Yarmuk in modern Syria.

638
Islamic forces conquer Jerusalem.

711
An Arab Muslim army conquers the Visigothic kingdom in Spain.

714–741
In the attempt to create a large army of knights on horseback, Charles Martel, a powerful Frankish nobleman, grants many "benefices" or "fiefs." This marks the expansion of the feudal system. On their manorial landholdings, fief holders exercise administrative power. In addition, they control the lives of most of Europe's agricultural peasants, or serfs.

725
The Byzantine emperor Leo III bans the use of icons in Eastern Christian churches and tries to do the same in the West. The following "iconoclastic" controversy lasts until 787.

732
Charles Martel's army defeats an invading Islamic army at Poitiers in France.

754
Pepin III of the Carolingian family is proclaimed king of the Franks by Pope Stephen II. The event creates the alliance between the papacy and the Frankish kings.

768
Charlemagne becomes king of the Franks.

775
A falsified document appears, the Donation of Constantine, which claims that the Roman Catholic Church is the true heir to the Roman Empire.

782
An Anglo-Saxon monk, Alcuin of York, is commissioned to run the Palace School at Charlemagne's court at Aachen. The event marks the Carolingian Renaissance, a rebirth of learning and culture.

793
Over two hundred years of Viking invasions begin with an attack on the monastery at Lindisfarne in Britain.

800
Charlemagne is crowned Holy Roman Emperor by Pope Leo III.

814
Charlemagne dies.

814
Under Charlemagne's successor, Louis the Pious, bishops and abbots are forced to swear oaths of feudal loyalty to the king. In turn they receive fiefs in the form of lands and church offices.

827
Muslims invade and conquer Sicily and harass the Christian kingdoms in Italy and France.

843
Charlemagne's kingdom, known as both the Kingdom of the Franks and the Holy Roman Empire, is partitioned into three separate kingdoms. The three kingdoms correspond roughly to France, Germany, and the Low Countries in between.

898–920
The Magyars invade Europe from central Asia. By the end of the 900s they take up Christianity and settle in the plain of the Danube River.

912
The Viking chieftan Rollo is converted to Christianity. He accepts the title of Duke of Normandy, located in northern France.

921
Swedish Vikings fight as mercenaries in the Byzantine army, after having reached Constantinople by way of the Russian river system.

ca. 1000
Viking settlers establish the colony of Vinland in North America, after having already settled Iceland and Greenland.

1054
The leaders of Roman Catholic Christianity and Eastern Orthodox Christianity, differing over both doctrine and religious authority, excommunicate one another. This schism between Western and Eastern Churches still exists.

1066
William of Normandy, Rollo's descendant as duke of Normandy, mounts a successful invasion of England known as the Norman Conquest.

1071
At the Battle of Manzikert, the Byzantine Empire suffers a defeat at the hands of the Seljuk Turks, a new Islamic power.

For Further Research

Books

Geoffrey Barraclough, *The Medieval Papacy*. New York: W.W. Norton and Co., 1968.

Johannes Brondsted, *The Vikings*. Baltimore: Penguin Books, 1971.

Robert Browning, *Justinian and Theodora*. London: Thames and Hudson, 1987.

William Ragsdale Cannon, *History of Christianity in the Middle Ages*. New York: Abingdon Press, 1960.

Peter Cramer, *Baptism and Change in the Early Middle Ages*. New York: Cambridge University Press, 1993.

Glanville Downey, *Constantinople in the Age of Justinian*. Norman: University of Oklahoma Press, 1960.

Katherine Fischer-Drew, ed., *The Barbarian Invasions: Catalyst of a New Order*. New York: Holt, Rinehart, and Winston, 1970.

Guy Fourquin, *Lordship and Feudalism in the Middle Ages*. London: Allen and Unwin, 1976.

Frances Gumley and Brian Redhead, *The Christian Centuries*. London: BBC Books, 1989.

P.J. Heather, *Goths and Romans*. Oxford, UK: Clarendon Press, 1991.

Patrick Howarth, *Attila, King of the Huns*. London: Constable, 1994.

Walter Kaegi, *Byzantium and the Decline of Rome*. Princeton, NJ: Princeton University Press, 1968.

Solomon Katz, *The Decline of Rome and the Rise of Medieval Europe*. Ithaca, NY: Cornell University Press, 1955.

Harold Lamb, *Constantinople: Birth of an Empire*. New York: Alfred A. Knopf, 1966.

C.H. Lawrence, *Medieval Monasticism: Forms of Religious Life in the Middle Ages*. London: Longman Press, 1989.

Jules LeBreton, *The History of the Early Church*. New York: Collier Books, 1962.

Harry Magoulias, *Byzantine Christianity: Emperor, Church, and the West*. Chicago: Rand McNally, 1970.

Rosamond McKitterick, *The Frankish Kingdom Under the Carolingians*. London: Longman Press, 1983.

Joan O'Grady, *Heresy, Heretical Truth, or Orthodoxy? A Study of Early Christian Heresies*. Shaftesbury, UK: Element Books, 1985.

Henri Pirenne, *Mohammad and Charlemagne*. London: George Allen and Unwin, 1939.

Susan Reynolds, *Fiefs and Vassals*. Oxford: Oxford University Press, 1994.

Jeffrey Richards, *The Popes and the Papacy in the Early Middle Ages, 476–752*. London: Routledge and Kegan Paul, 1979.

Carl Stephenson, *Medieval Feudalism*. Ithaca, NY: Cornell University Press, 1965.

Joseph R. Strayer, *Feudalism*. Huntington, NY: R.E. Krieger Publishing Co., 1979.

Hugh Trevor-Roper, *The Rise of Christian Europe*. London: Harcourt, Brace, and World, 1965.

Walter Ullman, *The Carolingian Renaissance and the Idea of Kingship*. London: Methuen, 1969.

Richard Winston, *Charlemagne: From the Hammer to the Cross*. New York: Vintage Books, 1954.

Periodicals

James Graham Campbell, "The Vikings in England," *History Today*, July 1982.

H.A. Drake, "Lambs Into Lions: Explaining Early Church Intolerance," *Past and Present*, November 1966.

Stephen Gero, "Byzantine Iconoclasm and Monachomachy," *Journal of Ecclesiastical History*, July 1977.

K.W. Harl, "Sacrifice and Pagan Belief in Fifth and Sixth Century Byzantium," *Past and Present*, August 1990.

Judith Herrin, "Historians and Their Times: The Byzantine Secrets of Procopius," *History Today*, August 1988.

Helge Ingstad, "Vinland Ruins Prove Vikings Found the New World," *National Geographic*, November 1964.

Robert Paul Jordan, "Viking Trail East," *National Geographic*, March 1985.

Karl Leyser, "Concepts of Europe in the Early and High Middle Ages," *Past and Present*, November 1992.

P.A.B. Llewelyn, "The Roman Church in the Seventh Century: The Legacy of Gregory I," *Journal of Ecclesiastical History*, October 1974.

Rosamond McKitterick, "Charles the Bald and the Image of Kingship," *History Today*, June 1988.

Klaus Randsborg, "Barbarians, Classical Antiquity, and the Rise of Western Europe," *Past and Present*, November 1992.

David S. Sefton, "Pope Hadrian I and the Fall of the Kingdom of the Lombards," *Catholic Historical Review*, April 1979.

Merle Severy, "The Byzantine Empire: Rome of the East," *National Geographic*, December 1983.

Brent D. Shaw, "The Family in Late Antiquity: The Experience of Augustine," *Past and Present*, May 1987.

—————, "Women and the Early Church," *History Today*, February 1994.

Chris Wickham, "The Other Transition: From the Ancient World to Feudalism," *Past and Present*, May 1984.

Walter J. Wilkins, "Submitting the Neck of Your Mind: Gregory the Great and Women of Power," *Catholic Historical Review*, October 1991.

Index

234 The Early Middle Ages